D1443063

DATE DUE

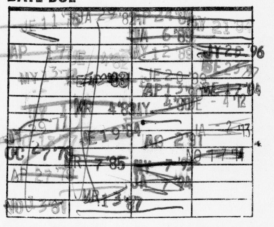

EXPLORING THE INNER WORLD

EXPLORING THE INNER WORLD

*A guidebook for personal growth
and renewal*

Tolbert McCarroll

THE JULIAN PRESS, INC.
Publishers • New York

Published by THE JULIAN PRESS, INC.
150 Fifth Avenue, New York, N.Y. 10011

The true profession
of man is to find his
way to himself.
Hermann Hesse

Dedicated
to
MARTI

CONTENTS

I

The Expedition and the Equipment

1

I LIVE IN four different worlds. In the first, a world of objects, I must be able to see myself as a thing and respect the natural forces governing things. More important, I must see the commonness between me and other things. The second world is a social one in which I have roles. I function as a parent, a teacher, a helper, or one who is asking for help. I see and even judge myself by how well I function in these roles. I look at others the same way. Can I make someone happy? Is he a good teacher for me? In the third world of "I and Thou" I see you as a person, as an individual. You do not have a social role. I am not asking what you can do for me. I see myself in you and feel you in me. The fourth world is the world of me. It is the most unfamiliar of the four worlds. As children most of us truly experience our own inner world, but as we grow older we lose contact. I fully experienced this world at the moment of birth and will probably again fully and solitarily experience it at the moment of my death. Between birth and death this world is unexplored territory to most of us.

The world of me has many titles. It has been variously described by numerous people. It is not a new world, nor is it a creature of contemporary psychology or any other academic discipline. The world of me has been called the unconscious, the soul, the divine spark, *puer aeternus*, or even a little elflike creature living in the pit of the stomach. Karen Horney calls this world "The real self, that essential inner force common to all human beings yet unique to each which is the deep source of growth" (1). We must journey to this inner world, but as R. D. Laing reminds us:

> As adults, we have forgotten most of our childhood, not only its contents but its flavor; as men of the world, we

hardly know of the existence of the inner world; we barely remember our dreams, and make little sense of them when we do; as for our bodies, we retain such sufficient provocative proprioceptive sensations to coordinate our movements and to insure the minimal requirements for bio-social survival—to register famine, signals for food, sex, defecation, sleep; beyond that, little or nothing. Our capacity to think, except in the service of what we are dangerously deluded into supposing is our self-interest and in conformity with common sense is pitifully limited; our capacity even to see, hear, touch, taste and smell is so shrouded in veils of mystification that an intense discipline of unlearning is necessary for anyone before one can begin to experience the world afresh, with innocence, truth and love (2).

A few years ago I acknowledged my inner world and began to travel there. At first I went as a tourist, dashing in and out and posing as a well-traveled expert. One day in a lonely mood I returned to my inner world and found a companion. "I meet him," goes the Buddhist saying, "but know not who he is, I converse with him, but do not know his name." My companion became a guide to the world of me. I found that the inner world was not a vacation land for tourists, but a school requiring self-discipline. I had first to become aware of me, and then to learn to live in the presence of me, to accept me, and to hear me. As I demonstrated to the teacher within that I was serious, that I would study, more and more lessons were open to me. The school has become a training place, a place of growth. I not only learn an awareness of me, but also receive help in solving my problems and realizing my potential. My teacher has gradually become a counselor.

I know that I am this place. I am the teacher and the

counselor. I can truly live in this inner world as I do in the other three worlds, but I have erected many obstacles along the roads. Many games and tricks are cultivated to convince ourselves that there is no inner world, that there is no road to it, that we already know what is there, or that we do not need it.

Carl G. Jung says of his voyage of self-exploration:

> The years when I was pursuing my inner images were the most important in my life—in them everything essential was decided. It all began then; the later details are only supplements and clarifications of the material that burst forth from the unconscious, and at first swamped me. It was the *prima materia* for a lifetime's work (3).

We can all benefit from such a voyage. I have to come to terms with the inner world in order to find contentment. There are many tools to help remove the obstructions on the road, and the following chapters are a manual on the use of these tools. The tools are not ends in themselves, but ways of exploring the inner world. I use these tools to chip away the accumulated debris covering the inner world, and as I use them they become old trusted friends. They produce fragments that are part of the picture of the inner world.

All the tools are avenues that lead to the same place. Each requires a special discipline, each has its own unique uses and limitations. By using a variety of tools, we can get a better picture of the inner world. In the familiar Buddhist fable three blind men attempt to describe an elephant after each explores a different part of the animal. This story was a parable used to explain man's attempt to define spiritual matters and applies equally well to the exploration of the self. If we allow ourselves more perspectives, we gain more awareness of our inner world and are able to experience more of that world.

The object of self-exploration is not to analyze, but to hear. There is a rich experience around you and inside of you. You are a rich experience, and it is necessary to become aware of this experience. To ask "why" is to set yourself an impossible task. You will be frustrated in two ways: You will not find the answer and you will stop the dynamic process of listening to your own experience. If there must be a question, it is not "why" but "what."

"All right, I'm aware, I hear my inner message, I've heard it before. What do I do with the information?" This question seems reasonable, but it is always premature. When you are truly aware, you will know what to do with the information. Or, more likely, you will have already experienced a change. To really hear the message is to hear the clues about what to do next.

Today we are talking a lot about self-investment, self-awareness, self-improvement. Everything in this book is encouraging self-exploration. There is a danger in these quests —the age-old problem of preoccupation with the self. It is as if a person is hypnotized while looking in a mirror. He focuses only on his image. He refuses to move, wanting more knowledge, more spirituality, more self. He is very conscious of the self. He is stuck. This demand for more self is not really self-exploration, it is going in circles. Self-awareness can turn into preoccupation with self. Thomas Merton describes such an individual when he writes:

> This brings with it an instinct to study themselves, to shape their lives, to remodel themselves, to tune and re-tune all their inner dispositions—and this results in full-time meditation and contemplation on *themselves*. They

may unfortunately find this so delightful and absorbing that they lose all interest in the invisible and unpredictable action of grace. In a word, they seek to build their own security, to avoid the *risk* and *dread* implied by submission to the unknown mystery of God's will (4).

What then is the way out of this dilemma? How can one study oneself and not become preoccupied with the self? A helpful suggestion comes from the thirteenth-century mystic, Meister Eckhart. "The truth is," he says, "that the more ourselves we are, the less self is in us." On the other side of the world, Dogen-zenji taught that "to study Buddhism is to study ourselves. To study ourselves is to forget ourselves."

We must enter into the center of ourselves and there we become no longer conscious of ourselves. The self-conscious person is indeed not a person who is studying himself too much but not enough. He prefers to stay at an early level of self-exploration instead of dropping deep within himself. As he begins to really hear himself he avoids the dramatic, the phony, the artificial, the mask—he becomes himself. He does not attempt to be anyone else. A man who is truly himself is not preoccupied with himself.

The journey to the inner world is not a ponderous one. It is frequently light and humorous. Above all, it is not a sacred affair. Self-exploration should be an ordinary part of everyday life, not an occasional dramatic turn-on. The quest and the tools themselves are as old as man. Many men have written of the experience. "The inner man must govern the outer," says Meister Eckhart. "You must," he tells us, "depart from all crowds and go back to the starting point, the core out of which you came." He sees this core, this inner world, as a castle. "Look and see: this little castle in the soul is exalted so high above every road . . . that God himself can not even . . . steal into it" (5).

Across the globe an unknown Zen monk writes, "He who sees not into his own nature sees not anything at all." St. John of the Cross describes the expedition to the inner world as a "venture of delight" (6). William Blake shares the awesome vision of his inner world in powerful poetry (7). Black Elk, the last great holy man of the Ogalala Sioux, urges us to act out with ceremonies the stories of the inner world to experience our inner strength (8). A twentieth-century Tibetan abbot advises:

> Whatever one does, whatever one tries to practice, is not aimed at achieving a higher state or at following some theory or ideal, but simply, without any object or ambition, trying to see what is here and now (9).

It is discouraging to think that I am the product of a cultural history that has created so much confusion, and that I myself have been the engineer who has obstructed my ability to hear myself. However, it is encouraging to know that the task to which I have dedicated myself is one that was natural to my ancestors and to the child who still resides within me. When I have truly accepted my inner world, there will be no difference between what is outer and inner.

II

The Journal

2

YOU ARE ON a voyage of self-exploration. You need a log to record the adventure. The journal is not a place for explaining, for asking or answering why. It is not a diary. It is a log.

THE LOG

On this quest the activities recorded are dreams, fantasy, art experiences, and similar events. The items are recorded in a simple manner with no comment, editing, or analysis (1). The journal is a record of what is; not what should be.

There are many other kinds of logs. The master on a ship decides what data to collect, what events to record in the ship's log.

The following excerpt from the *Journals of Henry David Thoreau* refers to the adventure of life around a small New England pond. Like any log, it is the author's quiet conversation with himself as a means of keeping in touch with the source of his strength.

JANUARY 3, 1858.

. . . *Going to the Andromeda Ponds, I was greeted by the warm, brown-red glow of the Andromeda calyculate toward the sun. I see where I have been through, the more reddish undersides apparently being turned up. It is long since a human friend has met me with such a glow.*

JANUARY 5.

. . . *Mr. Hosmer is loading hay in his barn. It is meadow-hay, and I am interested in it chiefly as a botanist. If meadow-hay is of less worth in the market, it is more interesting to the* poet . . . How completely a load of hay in the winter revives the memory of past summers! Summer in us is only a little dried like it. The rowen in Hosmer's barn has a finer and greener look than the first crop. And so the ferns in coal remind us of summer still longer past.

JANUARY 7.

The storm is over, and it is one of those beautiful winter mornings when a vapor is seen hanging in the air between the village and the woods . . .

I see some tree sparrows feeding on the fine grass seed above the snow, near the road on the hillside below the Dutch house. They are flitting along one at a time, their feet commonly sunk in the snow, uttering occasionally a low sweet warble and seemingly as happy there, and with this wintry prospect before them for the night and several months to come, as any man by his fireside . . .

JANUARY 9.

Snows again.

To Deep Cut. The wind is southwest, and the snow is very moist, with large flakes. Looking toward Trillium Wood, the nearer flakes appear to move quite swiftly, often making the impression of a continuous white line. They are also seen to move directly and nearly horizontally, but the more distant flakes appear to loiter in the air, as if uncertain how they will approach the earth, or even to cross the course of the former, and are always seen as simple and distinct flakes (2).

BEGINNING A JOURNAL

Obtain a good sized notebook (3). Artists' sketchbooks are inexpensive and ideal in every way. There is usually an embarrassing moment as you look at your new journal. How to start? We feel the first entry should be very impressive. Do not use the journal to impress yourself, and certainly not posterity. If nothing else works to break the mystique, rip out the first page. The journal is an existential joke book. It is a place to play, to be free and spontaneous. The journal is you—all of you, including the parts that are not introduced into polite society; the immature you, the dreamer, the child. The journal is the place where they all come together without invitation and without rejection. And you own whatever is there.

There is a haiku by Issa that belongs in the front of every journal:

> He who appears
> before you now—is the Toad
> of this Thicket (4).

Whatever comes, it's my thicket.

So far we have torn out the first page and put down an eighteenth-century haiku. Now what? There are many ways of beginning a journal. The following suggestions have worked for a number of people.

1. Commit yourself to doing a fantasy and recording it every day for at least two weeks. (See chapter III.)

2. Record any dreams that you remember. (See chapter IV.)

3. After the first week begin to put an art experience, either a picture or a doodle, into the journal each day. Commit yourself to do this for at least two weeks. (See chapter V.)

4. As other tools suggest themselves, commit yourself

to record these experiences for a definite number of days or weeks in addition to the events you are already recording.

5. Do not try to understand each thing that is recorded, but go back frequently and reread what you have written.

6. Set a definite time each day to work in your journal, such as when you wake up in the morning. If you remember a dream, record it. If not, then use a fantasy or art experience. After a week or so, add a second time of day. The period after work and before dinner is a good time for many people. In the beginning set a maximum time limit, such as fifteen minutes, for recording. The shorter the time, the harder it is to find excuses for not doing it. As you use your journal, you will discover how best to pursue your own unique relationship with your journal.

THE COMPANION

My journal is many things to me; above all, it is a companion. It helps me gain self-discipline and keeps my experiences alive.

Discipline is important in this quest. Inner messages are not given to the casual dilettante. Am I really trying to hear myself? This is the basic question. A glance through your journal will tell you whether you are only talking about self-exploration or are actually engaged in the process.

Many of the experiences logged in a journal have a short life span. By your writing them down, their duration is prolonged a few precious moments. The act of recording also allows you to regain some of your emotional involvement each time you return to what you have written.

Each experience is a piece in a puzzle. You could try to

work a jigsaw puzzle by using one piece and trying to deduce what the entire puzzle looks like, but it would waste considerable time in unproductive speculation. A better use of your energy and a clearer sense of the picture can be obtained by collecting as many pieces as possible. Each new piece gives additional meaning to the ones already collected. The journal is the table upon which to store and play with the pieces collected.

DIALOGUE

Frequently, we are able to hear several voices coming from the inner world. Usually these parts of our personality are not speaking to each other. My image is of two or more intense actors standing on a stage speaking to an audience, but never facing each other. When they are not speaking to each other, there is a tendency to repeat.

- *"I have a lot of work to do."*
        - *"I want to play."*
- *"I have got to get at my work."*
        - *"I need to play."*
- *"I must work."*
        - *"I must play."*

A great deal can happen when we encourage these voices to turn and talk to each other. Often they can work together. There are many techniques for encouraging the dialogue. One is to put a voice into each of your hands. Look at each hand in turn and speak for it. Keep the conversation going.

Often dialogue begins to develop naturally in your journal. Until it is recognized that there are two or more voices in an experience, it can be confusing. After you have worked in the journal for several months, use it as a place for dialogue. There is a simple way to stimulate this process. Put a record on the phonograph. Preferably it should be a record without words, and with unfamiliar music. An Asian or African record often works well. Set a definite period of time you are going to work, and write. Do not plan; do not stop until your time has elapsed. Do not edit or create; just write. You should see dialogue beginning.

After the journal becomes a frequent place for dialogue, you may find three or more voices coming into the conversation. This use of the journal encourages a necessary and highly enriching feeling of flowing. From original dogmatic statements of position evolves practical advice.

The following is a short dialogue from my own journal. This was written to music. I wrote rapidly.

- *Here I go again*
- *I am tight.*
  - *Let loose.*
- *I'm afraid.*
  - *Be yourself.*
- *Who the hell is that!*
  - *Now you are ok.*
  - *Keep going.*
- *da da dum dum da da dum dum*
  - *Follow you.*
  - *Lead you.*
  - *Now is the time.*

- For what?
- I reach within and give out.
                              - And you need nourishment.
- And I need nourishment.
- I'll ask.
                              - Don't ask—demand!
- Demand!

                    - Let's dance, around
                      we go hey ho.
                      Me, I'm all I need—
                      but I'm not all
                      I want!! When I don't
                      need you, I want you—
                flow flow flow flow flow flow
                      flow the rhythm.
                      flow the life.
                      flow with the River.
                flow flow flow flow flow flow

A JOURNAL

The following are excerpts from the journal of a young friend seven months pregnant with her first child. She and her husband had just moved to a new home outside San Francisco. The entries in this ten-day period are typical of the daily entries in her journal.

OCTOBER 1.

Wall fantasy: Walking along stone wall—low wooden door —opens into tunnel—dark, damp, cool; not unpleasant. Long tunnel. Finally begins to curve up—up and up—out at top of mountain—trees, sun. Nothing to do but lean back and bask in the sun. Feels good.

Island fantasy: *Sand, palm trees—feels plastic—turtle bowl —swim to edge, climb over—I'm on the kitchen counter, and I like it there.*

Globe fantasy: *In a globe—concentrating on the globe itself —clear, like being inside a floating soap bubble—in pearl—like evening air high above San Francisco—but anchored somehow.*

OCTOBER 2.

Dream last night: *I'm on the street with several professional bicycle riders, one of whom is a friend of mine. My friend invites me to a testimonial dinner in honor of the riders and some cafeteria workers. The dinner is addressed by a union official who makes a nasty remark about conscientious objectors. The audience cheers. I am incensed, and walk out muttering loudly.*

If I were a different person, what would I be doing?
Opening up to my new surroundings
Working on getting the house ready
Other necessary work
Keeping up in my exercises, vitamins, weight watching, etc.
Doing a meditation every morning
Helping my husband
Using and owning my strength

OCTOBER 3.

Dream: *I'm in the labor room at a clinic. There are several other women there too. One Latin lady has two small children with her. She's clutching her stomach and throwing herself around. I hadn't felt prepared, but my labor is going easily, and I'm remembering to breathe properly . . .*

OCTOBER 4.

Dream: *I have to take care of a wolf for a day. The wolf is very friendly, but treacherous. It looks like a Doberman pinscher. I get it into the garage, feed it, pet it; then lock it in. Later I explain to someone how important it is not to let the wolf out. Finally someone comes to take over, and I am amazed at how matter-of-fact and unafraid this person is with the wolf.*

I am in an upstairs room with someone. We look out the window and see a brown Irish setter levitating above the telephone wires. We call it, and it comes in the window . . .

OCTOBER 5.

Dream: *I buy a red sweater in a department store, and a white one to wear under it. The girls in the jewelry section keep rearranging the merchandise, and I can't understand what they're doing.*

I learn that babies have to have lots of different colors of bibs (sensory stimulation) or they become apathetic . . .

OCTOBER 6.

Dream: *I've been invited to Lyn's for dinner, but we're having something good at home and I don't really want to go. In the end I decide to go and not hurt her feelings . . .*

OCTOBER 7.

Dream fragments: *Mary is angry because we took a list of jobs with us.*

I find out that my mother's genealogy is much more impressive than my father's . . .

OCTOBER 8.

Dream fragments: *Seeing Dr. Allan again, deciding he's not the Dr. for me.*

Choosing between stepmother and an older woman for my father; explaining why.

I am facing an exact replica of me who puts her hands on my shoulders and says, "You start here. You start where you are ..."

OCTOBER 9.

Stream fantasy: *Start as a mountain spring, clear, small pool. Then become a medium-sized, fairly slow-moving, calm-surfaced stream running between banks of autumn leaves. I wonder how I got there, see tumbling rapidly down stony channels; white water. Then branch many times, become small runnels that don't seem to be coming back together. Sense river in distance ...*

OCTOBER 10.

Dream: *Impending natural or man-made catastrophe. Have to leave where we're living. Howard leaves; we're supposed to get together later. I'm afraid we won't be able to find each other. I go with some other people. We pass scenes of disaster, come to a large house that looks reasonably safe, decide to stay there. I notice hip music on the stereo; what food's in the refrigerator. I'm going to fix us something to eat. Putting away the food we've brought, keeping it on separate shelves from the owner's food. Another chick starts to cook something out of things she's found on the stove in a large pan. She adds water and starts to heat. I stop her because some of the ingredients are still in their bottles, and there's a steam iron in the pan*

that doesn't belong at all. Otherwise the ingredients are of
good quality. Then I put on a Baez record, "One Day At a
Time." A girl says she doesn't much like Baez. But I leave it
on, and by the last selection ("You Make Me So Happy" by
Blood, Sweat and Tears) even she is impressed. I'm glad that
we are getting together again. I think, now I can borrow her
sewing machine, but reject the thought as unworthy. Then
Howard and I are trying to make love, but strangers keep coming through our bedroom to use the bathroom. It's morning;
we want to stay in bed. The baby is born.

   Writing to Music: Orient/samurai/cherry blossoms/don't
trust/unhappy/want to be somewhere else/out of place
   Peaceful
   Autumn leaves/falling/drifting/death/solemn/procession
   Rhythmic dance/sexual/humorous/uncontrolled/head loll-
ing/sweat glistening
   It's right. Here I am. Foot planted. Syncopation. Rainstorm.
Landslide. Wet earth.

   Seed fantasy: Concentrating on insides, convolutions. Stuck
there. Start to grow. Explode! Up and up and up . . . Sunflower,
nodding, swaying, feeling sun. Sigh of completion.

WHY BOTHER?

   The disciplines of growth are demanding. Its rewards
are not always immediate. Why do it? That is a difficult
question. If a person is not committed to his own growth,
there is no reason to undertake this journey. If you are
committed, then you explore your inner world simply because it is a necessary part of you.

It is not always easy to be ourselves. The first step is really to hear what is going on with us. The masks we wear for the benefit of others often deceive us as well. It is important that we learn to be ourselves. We do this by stopping the attempt to be somebody else. There is a wise biblical proverb:

"Drink the water of thy own well" (5).

You must drink your own water, be it bitter or sweet. You must be yourself. If you want to change or grow, you have to accept where you are and be who you are.

The wisdom for growth is within us. Once we have learned really to listen to ourselves we can hear suggestions for our next step. Sometimes there is pain. The wild storms of winter are a necessary preliminary for spring's beauty. Just as bodily discomfort can tell us when we have broken nature's rhythm, the pain in the heart can be a beacon showing us the next step on our journey.

It is through the discipline of keeping a journal that I learn to become me. Without this inner journey I feel incomplete and lonely. In the outer part of my experience I am handling things. I am conscious of all the "oughts" and "shoulds" of life. This is not enough. I want to hear from that part of me that never changes and feel those parts that change every second. It feels good to be me and the more me I am the less conscious I am of me.

Each of us is a necessary part of a long story. It would have been nice if we had been taught our place in the story when we were young children, but a while back it seems as if everyone forgot the story. So we all grew up wondering about our value and our worth. We search for a place where we can belong. Now when we are older and it is harder, we must learn that our value is in being who we are and that we belong here. It is through my journal that I can begin to hear my own story and to search for my part in the story of life (6).

The following dreams and comments concern a person who found her place through learning to listen to her inner world.

Anne was a fairly ordinary young woman. She had been drifting around before beginning the process of self-exploration. She was a nurse. In 1971 Anne came to a group that focused on improving interpersonal communication. She came because someone she met suggested it. Her approach to life and to the group was fairly casual. The group was being facilitated by a young man who was dying of cancer and who had chosen to spend his last year in intensive self-exploration. This young man, who is called Damian in these dreams, died in the summer of 1971. Anne was not particularly close to Damian, but during the last weeks of his life she stayed around him. She would sit with him in silence. He appreciated her presence. It was obvious that Anne was deeply impressed by something Damian had that she felt she lacked. It was as if for the first time in her life she was really attempting to listen. After Damian's death she decided to devote her full time to pursuing her personal and spiritual growth. All this time she was primarily being guided by a counselor who is called Thomas in her dreams.

She began to keep a journal in the fall of 1971. Anne was likable and rather quiet. Under the surface there was a lot of stubbornness and fear. She was afraid of being pushed and was always trying to find reasons for delaying taking steps. This is the first dream that she recorded in her journal:

OCTOBER 3, 1971.
I am in my apartment. I am by myself. I am wearing a long dress. I hear a knock at the door. I answer the door and it is Cal. He scares me. He looks very intense. He does not say anything. He walks in and points a gun at me. I have tears in my eyes. He tells me he is going to shoot. It is because I am destroying everything. He says I am always taking from everybody and never giving. I take from Thomas, Mary, and William, and he is not going to let me hurt him. I tell him that I want to be light. I do not have a sense of knowing what is going on.

During the next year Anne would frequently take a big step forward in her growth followed by a half step backward. She was still stubborn and closed, but beginning to feel her strength. Anne's self-centeredness was becoming more obvious. She wanted to grow, but she was not willing to endure much discomfort. Her normal pattern was to travel around and to be a visitor. She had never put down roots. Whenever the going got tough she wanted to take off. There were increasingly strong indications that within her was a call to a simple and deeply committed spiritual life.

APRIL 21, 1972.
I am in a big house. There are several storeys. The house is built in a circular fashion. I am on the second floor. There is a bannister that goes around in a circle with doors all the way round. I start to count. I remember there are quite a few. I am leaning over the bannister and I can see the main floor. There is a marble floor with a design. It is a mandala. I am focused

on it. I feel hypnotized. I hear bells ringing. I start walking. I am in somewhat of a daze. I go into a room. I open the door and enter the room. It is huge. I descend three stairs. It is very quiet in there. There are a few people. Maybe three people sitting on the floor. It is a meditation room. It is a huge room. I am overwhelmed. I become sharper and more aware of where I am, as if I woke up.

The room is like a Greek palace. Pillars, people in simple robes, white and purple. I go into a room and change into a purple robe. The robe feels soft and silky. I am wearing nothing else. I want to describe this room. I feel like I have been here before. But also I am awed by newness.

I am now carrying a candle and descending the stairs. I go down nine stairs. The fact that it is nine is special—has some special meaning. I am impressed. As I walk down I move toward the center. I am distracted by the design of the floor. It is like a mosaic. There are seats or cushions made of velvet. I am seated in one. I feel the seat with my hands. I feel special, humble, and respectful looking at something.

Then someone begins to speak. A strong voice. I look around to see who it is. I don't see anyone. Then I am petrified. The voice is coming from inside me. I am motionless— scared, but I listen. The voice says, "Sit still. There is a place. Stars will shine and flowers grow. Men grow old. Babies will move the earth, and you will be searching. Candles melt. Men grow old. Let the star shine." I am worried. I want to remember the words. I want to stay. I move. I want to move. I feel something inside—blood rushing around. I am into myself.

Someone comes up to where I am and bows and kisses me upon both cheeks, closes both eyes, and raises my body. I go with what is going on. It is a man with a beard. He has a brown robe on. I am standing now with my eyes closed. He is touching me no longer. I stand there for a long time.

Hearing these voices within her did not make Anne's life any more pleasant. She was still the same stubborn and resistant person as before. If anything, knowing that a part of her was longing to move in the direction reflected in her dream was a burden and caused a conflict.

Then in the fall of 1972 something began to happen. She made a choice to move and to risk and she began to take courageous steps. She became much less self-centered and much more moving, flowing, open, honest, and direct.

AUGUST 26, 1972.

I am fixing flowers in vases. There are a lot of flowers on the floor. I think of friends, old and new. I am waiting for some friends to come by. People from the past. I am with someone.

(There is a shift)

I am in someone's house. There are a lot of people. I know some of them. I see a man I know. He says, "I know how to play the recorder," but he has this equipment on his head. I lay down on the couch to listen. I realize that I could die tomorrow and no one would care. Someone says no matter where you go you will always wear a mask. I am scared. I want to do something.

In the weeks that follow that dream Anne became alive in a way that she had never experienced before in her life. She dropped almost all her games and masks. But at a crucial moment she began the old seesaw game of stepping forward and then stepping back. The difference now was that Anne was spending an hour or more each day in working on her journal and she had learned to listen to her inner world for advice. There was a recurring theme that her happiness lay in getting outside herself, and in making some kind of commitment about what she was going to do in her life.

NOVEMBER 28, 1972.

There is something about being powerful. My body feels explosive.

(*There is a shift*)

I am in Thomas's office. I am talking and flowing. I realize what I am doing. I am pulling away. There is some conflict inside me about going all the way. Thomas starts to yell. I yell back. I realize what I am doing. I move toward Thomas with anger. I attack. I am in pain. I want to hit him. I feel pierced. I am crying. I am holding him, grabbing him. I move from anger and I embrace him. I feel deep sadness. Thomas says something. I run out of his office. I hear his voice loud. I go for the door and run up the stairs to the meditation room. I close the door. I want quiet, alone. I feel dark.

(*There is a shift*)

I am traveling in Europe. I can speak French. I go to Africa to the place of the Bushmen. I keep close contact with Thomas and Mary. I am writing a journal, a book. I continue with my daily discipline. While away I learn that I have a critical disease. I let Thomas know. I return and end the rest of my life in quiet and alone. I live in a small place. I die young and peaceful.

In that dream Anne saw many things. One of them was the danger of the old pattern of avoidance. She was truly learning to listen to her dreams and she was changing her life in accordance with what she heard. During this time she was exciting to be with and she was taking many more steps forward than backward.

Finally, there came a moment in which she realized that she had to commit herself to something in order to continue her growth. She was very attracted to the spiritual path of Damian, Thomas, and their friends. If only she could take that step without giving up her selfishness and her ability just to take off when she felt like it. She wanted to delay making the decision. She longed to be a carefree tourist again.

JANUARY 11, 1973.

I am in Germany. I am running across a field. It is open country. I am going somewhere. There is a lot of green. I am a lion. I am running very fast. I feel watched or that someone is after me. I am a lion with golden fur. There is someone else with me—a man—a tin soldier. He gets caught. I run very fast across the open fields. There are trees at the other end of the field. I see a building. It is white and on the other side. I run for it and go right in. I thought that it was an office building. I walk down the hall. I see a door open and a bed inside. I am greeted by a man. He sees I am a lion, but he does not draw back. He accepts me and I go in. His wife and daughter are there. He is drinking rum. He likes it. I step toward the window and see beautiful countryside. A lot of castlelike buildings. I keep looking. I see some bricklike buildings. I am very excited. The girl starts to explain to me what things are. The man pours me a drink. I tell him that I have never had rum before. It seems like a lot in a glass. The girl is very warm. She says something about not liking rum.

(There is a shift)

The girl starts to show me movies. I remember seeing their boat. The pictures all look like they are painted, but they are photographs, but rough. The wife reminds me of Mrs. Donovan. The daughter is very nice. Things look clear. There is a close feeling. The pictures tell the story. I think they are on a

fishing journey. *There is a fishing reel. The girl says what kind
it is and then looks at the picture and it is written on the side
of the rod. She was right. I feel good for her. The color in the
picture is good. I remember yellows—bright warm colors.*
            (*There is a shift*)
    *I am in a forest. I leave the forest and go into a clearing.
I feel exposed. I feel scared. I run around. I am a lion or dressed
as a lion. I am not sure. I have a friend and companion with
me who doesn't run as well as I do. I do for myself.*

In that dream Anne experienced both the joy and the
hollowness of the tourist approach to life. It is as if her inner
world has said, "You are desirous of living this way—tonight
let's really experience what it would be like." She knew that
she had to do something else, but what? A few days later
she dreamed of Jim, a colleague, who had interrupted his
period of spiritual training to go off traveling in search of
freedom.

JANUARY 14, 1973.
    *Jim comes back. He is thinner, paler; he looks older. He
talks about how he traveled with his wife and son through
Texas and somewhere else and they all got busted. And he
talks about a young girl's cat that got thrown out on a street
and hurt. The girl cried.*
            (*There is a shift*)
    *We are in a circle. Thomas is talking. Jim is there. They are
planning groups. Thomas hands me a colored key. I drop it.
He says something about "Anne, that is your problem, you
don't listen." There are other people there. Jim talks. Thomas
comes over and starts talking to me. A girl walks in, in a long
dress, kind of casual. I know her. Thomas says she teaches the
English class. He asks if I thought I could teach it.*

(There is a shift)
I am in a stall-like bathroom. There is defecation on the floor covered over with some stuff like seeds.
(There is a shift)
I am in the desert in a house. Not my house. It belongs to some foreigners. They have two kids. They don't like me. Someone starts to shoot at me. Something about wanting me to teach one of them.
(There is a shift)
I am outside on a ranch. There are horses. I am outside the fence. It is dark. Someone is after me with a gun. I am not sure what is going on. The children like me; the father is complaining about something.
(There is a shift)
I see Jim. He is thin, pale. His beard has been removed. I hug him. He doesn't respond. He walks off. I feel sad.
(There is a shift)
Thomas is smiling.

Anne could hear a lot of things in this dream, but what was this key that Thomas was handing her and that she dropped. She felt it had something to do with making the final commitment to her own growth, and to start putting down some kind of roots. There was no question about what she wanted to do. She wanted to join the spiritual community that Damian and Thomas were a part of, in order to continue her growth and to work with others to build something. There was no specific pressure on her to do this, as there were many studying with Thomas and others who were on quite different paths that did not lead to joining this community. Nonetheless, she felt inside her a pull toward that particular way of life. That was not the problem. The act of commitment itself was the stumbling block. She was withholding making any kind of decision, acting as if she needed more data, more information, and more time to think about it.

JANUARY 27, 1973.
   My face is beautiful. I am radiating. My hair is pulled back.
         (There is a shift)
   I am outside in a grove surrounded by many tall trees. They are beautiful. I am walking around.
         (There is a shift)
   I am on all fours walking. I feel like a dog with my head down. I am in the desert. It is very hot. I continue to walk on all fours.
         (There is a shift)
   I am at St. Teresa's inside the church. A strong feeling comes over me, in me. I feel radiant. I am walking up the aisle. I feel part of all my past and very close to the church. I focus on the crucifix. I feel happy and joyful. I am smiling. The crucifix talks. "You are at home." I hear, I don't hear. I keep on going.

After the dream Anne knew that the time was now. She must either say yes or no. There could be no more acting as if she didn't hear something that she heard.

Then Anne said yes. She let go of her caution. It was as if a ton of baggage was lifted. She went through a major spiritual experience and renewal. It was as if she looked at the world for the first time. She felt clear and warm. Anne said that her heart felt on fire. She truly felt free.

Here are a couple of her dreams during that time.

FEBRUARY 1, 1973.

I am floating in air. I am in a different place. There is a bright light all around me and through me.

FEBRUARY 4, 1973.

I am doing something. Donald is there.

(There is a shift)

Something about going into the other room. It is a better room.

(There is a shift)

There are lots of rooms. People are in the rooms. I am in a house. Virginia is doing something there. I get matches. They are good ones. They light quickly. Each room has specific things going on in it. Each room is designated. I go from room to room seeing different people I know. I am responsible for the flow of things in this house. I have my own room.

(There is a shift)

There are kids around. Someone gives me something. It is wrapped up. I have a strong feeling of Virginia being around me or involved with this project.

(There is a shift)

I feel excited.

(There is a shift)

I have a sense of permanency—of knowing what I want—of being able to tell the future—of feeling sure—of feeling light.

When someone asked Anne what had happened to her she said, "I have bloomed." The shy, closed, sullen person had become open, joyful, and strong. She was extremely direct and honest. Her affect on people around her was enormous. To be with her was to sense that time and space stood still. She shot quickly to the essence of things. Great warmth filled her. All of this had come about by listening inside and learning who she really was and becoming that person.

FEBRUARY 6, 1973.

Carolyn is swimming. Things look very fancy. There is a fancy pool. Her mother is directing her. I am waiting to get in. I have to wait in line. The place is crowded. I get in and then realize that I am not in the pool alone. It is very crowded. I have to get out.

(There is a shift)

I am in a fancy cafe or dining area. I remember Eleanor, Lynn, Carlotta, and Carolyn and myself. We are sitting at a small table. A lady brings a big tray with fancy desserts and cakes. I remember what everyone else got. I picked one. Eleanor took two. I wasn't surprised. I was surprised at the one that Lynn chose. It was so plain. I did not eat.

(There is a shift)

I don't want to pretend any more. I am getting what I want. I am me!

(There is a shift)

I am walking. My dreams are all coming true. They are all one. I step in and out. It doesn't matter which way.

(There is a shift)

There is a desert. I am walking in the desert. I see the flowering cactus.

(There is a shift)

I am surrounded by light. It radiates. The light and I are one wherever I go.

(There is a shift)

I am at the Zen Center bowing and saying, "Thank you." I am in the library. I buy a book.

(*There is a shift*)

I am sitting. My back is straight. I feel tall and straight.

(*There is a shift*)

I see Thomas.

(*There is a shift*)

I am on the ground rolling, laughing, and laughing.

(*There is a shift*)

Something about being stoned. I feel uneasy. Feel mixed.

(*There is a shift*)

I feel very intense.

(*There is a shift*)

Something is going on. I feel wavelike motions inside, flowing, moving, powerful, higher, the waves are forceful.

(*There is a shift*)

I am with Damian. He is dead. He is alive. He is cold and hot. He says something about not pretending. I feel teary. He says, "Give it all. I want all of you—ALL!" It echoes all the time. His spirit moves inside me. He is inside me. I am purple. I make something purple. I am Damian. Damian is me—all one. "You are unfinished. You have more to give. Do it. You know what you want." I look inside me. I am lit up and inside me is a tree only I can see. The tree is bare, young, and strong.

(*There is a shift*)

I am at a table. The table is special and then again it is not special. I am sitting with Thomas, a Japanese man who is older, with glasses, a man in robes who I think is from India, another westerner, and myself. We are sitting at a square wooden table. It is very intense. Listening is most important. The table is small, so we touch. It is natural and no big deal.

Around us is a circle, a circle of people. I know the people. William and Mary are there. This is a very important time. It is a ceremony, a consecration or something. I know what it is.

We are an Order, an accepted Order. There is quiet. It is a beginning, a christening of the world. It is the beginning. We are named. There is a blessing. The doors open.

(There is a shift)

I am in the country in a monastery, feeling alive, working, with lots of energy. There is a round dome building. I get up at five in the morning. I walk to the dome building. We chant. We meditate. There is a circle. There is a loud chant. People are wearing hooded gowns. We are walking back. There are a lot of people. We go to the eating room. There are long wooden tables. We eat breakfast. There is great joy. I am the cook on this day. We eat bread, cheese, eggs. There is happiness. There is a community. There is lots of land and many individual people live there. People at all levels.

There is a three-story building where kids live. They are awake. Everyone is awake. We work. I work. During the day. It is easy for me to be quiet a lot. There are cows and horses. I go to the ocean. I walk in the ocean. I am wearing sandals. My hands are in my robe. I run. I run hard. I am at the shore. There are waves. There is a dog at my side, an Irish setter. I see William. We hug. I love him. I ride a horse very fast.

(There is a shift)

There are barns and chickens and pigs.

(There is a shift)

There is a red building, a school. It is one big room. Mary is there.

(There is a shift)

I am sitting with a group of people. It is a medical setting. Andrew is there.

(There is a shift)

I feel a shaking. There is a whole layout of buildings. Work is very important. Every day is important. I am here. I live in a separate place only temporarily. I am in the one-room building wearing only a robe. I am not me. I am not me for me. I am part of something. I feel intense. I feel quiet. I am wearing brown. I am part of everything. There is a pillow, a candle, and one flower in this room. One window with four panes. I am stepping back from the world, from everything, from myself. I am not alone. I am not separate. I am very joyful. I am happy. I feel part of history. There are trees around. It is before dawn. I awake.

(There is a shift)

I look out the window. A bird on the branch is singing. I am the bird. The bird is me. I am not there. I am light. I am a traveling light. There is no sense of time or anything.

(There is a shift)

I am eating from a bowl.

(There is a shift)

I know no other way.

(There is a shift)

I see Thomas. He is older. I visit him. He is in another building, alone, writing, very quiet. There is a close, warm, tender feeling. He says nothing. Nothing happens. I feel part of him. I feel a deep connection.

(There is a shift)

I am on the ground laughing. More than laughing. I am on another level, another, all time is now, now—everything comes together.

(There is a shift)

I stay in this place for a period of time—a week—a month—I am outside. I am part of the community. I feel a flowing. I feel very warm. I am running with the children. Yeah! Yeah!

(There is a shift)

I am older. I spend a lot of time alone. I am me and yet not me. I feel like an instrument. I write but it is not really me writing.

(There is a shift)
I see Mary. I like seeing Mary. Our eyes meet. I feel intense.
We are happy. We hug. She sees me.
(There is a shift)
I think of Narcissus. I am thin yet strong. I eat once a day
yet I am not hungry.
(There is a shift)
Things are the same. Things are not the same. I feel like I
don't have a body. I feel like I have a body. I am a flower. I am
a fire.

Each person must find his own home. Anne found hers. She had learned to listen, be guided, and to act upon what she experienced in her inner world. There was much pain at the time of planting and much joy at the time of harvest. That is what the hours, months, and years of self-exploration are all about. Anne's own reaction was "There is more; there is lots more."

A Shaker saying sums up the process in a few words:

OPEN THE WINDOWS
AND THE DOORS AND RECEIVE
WHOMSOEVER IS SENT.

III

Inner Imagery

3

IT IS IMPORTANT to find at least partial answers to the basic questions: What do I want? Who am I? How can I grow and change? If I just use my intellect in the search for the answers I will often hear only what I should want or should be; comfortable answers with moralistic sermons and judgments.

There is a way to come directly in contact with the richness of my whole being. I use a structure for a story or fantasy to which my inner self responds quickly before my head can control or edit the message. I simply look at what has come to the inner eye of my imagination in the fantasy. The inner imagery is a parable, a story that illustrates something of importance to me. I should not try to understand or analyze the parable, but become as fully aware of it as I can.

Inner imagery is often confused with three other activities: (1) It is not a form of literary construction in which I begin with a few ideas and build something for somebody to see and like. I do not make up a story. (2) It is not a group fantasy that helps members of a group hear and relate better to each other by creating a common fantasy. The group fantasy brings into focus what is common between us. (3) It is not a guided daydream such as those used by spiritual or psychological counselors. In this method a guide sets a scene and directs you through a detailed experience to let you see a problem, learn a truth, or give feedback to the guide.

THE PROCESS

A fantasy is like a wise thermometer that not only tells my temperature but also makes suggestions. It is a tool for gaining an awareness of my personal growth process. However, a contrived or invented story will not give clear information about my spiritual or emotional temperature. It requires spontaneous responses. This problem can be overcome by imposing a structure, a partial story line, to which you react quickly. A number of these structures are suggested at the end of this chapter.

The structure does not produce an image. More accurately it can be said to remove distractions. Suppose you are listening to an orchestra and there is a child sitting next to you who is blowing a whistle. Removing the whistle does not create the music, it lets you hear it. A fantasy structure unplugs the whistling parts of ourselves for a moment and lets us hear our quieter parts.

Get all the parts of a fantasy structure in mind before beginning, so that the fantasy can proceed at its own pace. When you listen to or read the structure, you may not completely understand it. Do not try to clarify the instructions. To clarify is to control. It is important to move quickly to overcome the tendency to edit or censor your reactions. Whatever you hear or read, react to it. Many strong fantasy experiences have resulted from a misunderstanding of the structure. For the same reason it is important to be aware of your first images or flashes and not to reject what comes because it was not good enough.

After selecting a particular structure, close your eyes and have the fantasy. It may happen all at once or it may take some time. People who are just beginning to use this tool often have fantasies that take from two to three minutes. The time for the fantasy usually decreases as you work with the method.

In the beginning what is spontaneous and what is constructed are hard to keep separated, but with each fantasy experience it becomes easier to be aware of the difference. When the fantasy feels over or when you believe you are making things happen, open your eyes.

Record the fantasy by writing it down without comment, analysis, or other editing. Write it as a story; something that happened. Your fantasy is seldom a complete and smooth story. It may seem only a fragment. Whatever you have, it's enough to work with.

As with all tools, we learn subtle lessons as we use them. For some there is a difference in the fantasy between seeing themselves and being themselves. Others learn to watch for what is not there. Skills of this sort are usually learned through the fantasy experience itself.

There are many symbols in fantasies. It is important to discard any concept of a universal meaning for symbols. You and I may both have a dream or fantasy with an orange ball. To me it may be an invitation to play and to you it may give a feeling of aimless wandering. Symbols have highly personal connotations that change even from one day to the next.

THE EXPERIENCE

Try using the fantasy tool now. It will help in understanding what follows.

Use the structure in the next paragraph. Close your eyes. Let things happen. When the fantasy ends or when you suspect you are controlling or constructing, stop. Write the fantasy down in a simple fashion without explanation or analysis. Write the fantasy as if you were telling a story to a child.

You are walking along the side of a wall. There is a way through or over the wall. On the other side is something you need or want. Find it and bring it back.

Consider that you asked yourself to tell a story about a wall. What happened is that you have been told a story with a message about where you are, what you want, or something of interest or importance. View it as a story. Do not analyze it or try to figure it out. To figure it out is to attempt to control it and control may destroy the message.

After you have done a number of these wall fantasies, the variations will help you be aware of the story of each fantasy. Sometimes it is not the details but the approach that contains the message. The story can be indirect, complex, frustrating, joyful, or humorous. At other times the impact is in the details.

Another way of working with inner imagery is to hear other people's fantasies. Each fantasy gives dimension to your own. Imagine that you are in a group of ten people, all of whom have just had wall fantasies. Read your fantasy again and listen to the other fantasies.

There is a long, long, long wall. Probably there is a way through, but it is too far to walk. I pull out a stone, make a hole, and go through the wall. The land is barren. I find a big leafless tree. There is a big fat bird in the tree. I grab him. He yells and flaps his wings. I soothe the bird, and put him under my arm and take him back through the wall.

I am skipping along a wall. I go through an open door and find a big steel disc. It is a shield. I am happy. I take it to the other side of the wall and sleep under it. I have a nice feeling of being taken care of.

The wall is low. I can see over it. On the other side is a meadow. I find a gate, throw the doors wide open and walk in. There is a tree full of light. I go back to the wall and knock it down. Then I return and look at the tree.

The wall is very tall. It is dark and barren on this side. I can not find a way through. There is a gate, but I can not open it. Finally I find a crack in the wall and I squeeze through. On the other side are guards. I hide. There is a candle. I steal it and sneak back through.

The wall is a high medieval battlement. A real iron gate. I pound and demand to be let in. Nothing happens. Beside the door is an opening. I walk through and find an empty bottle. I bring it back. I do not know what to do with it.

The wall is stone. There is a red ball on top. I do not like it, but I keep looking at it. I climb up and look at the ball. I am supposed to get something. I climb down and find a flower. I look back at the wall. I climb back up. The flower is crushed as I climb. I get back on top of the wall and look at the ball. I sit down and stay on the wall.

I am hurrying down a dark, damp street. A high brick wall blocks my way. I am frightened and anxious to get over the wall. I climb a ladder up the side of a building and step over the wall. I cannot see what is on the other side. I jump and roll in an open field. I feel exposed and vulnerable like on the wrong side of the Berlin Wall. I crouch and run to some trees. I begin to feel safe—able to face the dangers. I find a plain, poor shack and go inside. I go to the kitchen and find an apple pie. I take it and work my way back to the wall. I raise the pie up on a rope to the top of the wall, then climb up the rope, take the pie, and cross to the other side. I am not afraid in the street now.

The wall is made of eyes all looking at me. They are frightening and repulsive. The wall is a low mound so I step over it fairly easily. Then I see only my bare feet and the bottoms of my jeans going along the ground. My feet come to some thick grass. Gradually I realize it is fur and I am climbing an animal's back. Then I am sitting on the shoulders of a huge dog. I grab a fold of loose skin and he begins to run. We streak through the air and back over the wall and keep on going.

I just see part of the wall. It is bright orange and bumpy. I come to an orange grill gate. I have a hard time seeing what is inside. I try several times to make it out. Next thing I know I am inside and a man in a black coat swings me into the air. I come around like a boomerang and land where I was before. Then he takes me by the foot and swings me around and around over his head. As he lets go I realize he is George Washington. I become a silhouette riding a horse through the sky yelling, "The British are coming! The British are coming!" (1)

Read your own fantasy again. There will be a sharper perspective. After listening to other fantasies, you may hear your story better.

For me the message from fantasy is often sharp, even crude in its insistence. It is like two children in a horse costume. "I'll be the one back here in the dark. You can be the one looking out and deciding where we go, but I do ask a few things, and if we are going to work together you have got to listen to me. Now listen to me!" The attitude of the child in back resembles the messages from my inner world.

STRUCTURES

There are a large number of structures or triggering devices similar to the wall fantasy. Persons who use fantasy a great deal will gradually begin to evolve their own situations and stimulations. One of the most common is the following:

Random. *Decide to have a fantasy experience and let your eye quickly fall on an object. Be this object. Close your eyes and say to yourself, I am a glass, I am a book, I am a ball. Have the fantasy.*

Random fantasy is often difficult in the beginning. This is particularly true if you have a tendency to construct stories intellectually instead of experiencing a message.

The following are a number of structures that have worked for many people (2).

Fantasies defy classification. A particular situation may have been selected to bring out a certain piece of information, but something far different happens during the actual fantasy. If you restrict your listening, you may miss a much richer experience.

It is helpful to use one of the following structures several times on different occasions before going on to another. Do not analyze what happens. Let the fantasy have its own life. The message can be impeded by too many why's.

Wall. *You are walking along the side of a wall. There is a way over or through the wall. On the other side is something you need or want. Find it and bring it back.*

Box. A package has come for you. The package is in a room. Go into the room, unwrap the box, and open it.

Wise Man. Quickly formulate a question about something that is important to you. There is a wise man on top of a mountain. Go up the mountain, find the man, ask your question, and listen.

Sea Monster. Go to a beach. Equip yourself with everything you need to go to the bottom of the sea, including a magic wand. Go to the bottom of the sea. Look around. You will find a monster. Touch him with your wand and he will be immobilized. Explore the place where he lives. Bring the monster back to the shore. With the wand change the monster into anything you want him to be. (This is a good structure if there have been a series of heavy and serious messages, and you suspect you have been editing or taking yourself too seriously.)

Totem. You are in a clearing. Animals come to you. Construct a totem by putting them on top of each other.

Planet. You are a planet in orbit around a sun. Be aware of what you are doing.

Island. You are on an island. Get to the mainland.

Different Ages. This is a series of nine fantasies. You are born. You are nine. You are fifteen. You are twenty-two. You are your present age. You are one year older. You are ten years older. You are twenty years older. It is the last day of your life.

Statue. You are a statue. (After recording this fantasy, assume the posture of the statue in your fantasy and experience being the statue. Then record how you felt.)

House. You have all the materials and skills necessary to build your own house (or temple or garden). Record the fantasy by drawing the plan.

Castle. You are walking and come upon a castle. Enter it.

Seed. You are a seed. Grow.

Globe. You are in a clear globe. The globe fills with color, and then the color empties out of the globe.

Flag. Design your personal flag or banner. Record the fantasy by drawing it.

Stream. You are a stream. Travel along to the ocean.

Treasure map. Picture a map showing a hidden treasure. Now draw it.

Ship. You are on a ship.

Circle. You are sitting in a circle of people. There is a candle in the center. Go to the center, pick up the candle, and go back to your place in the circle. After a while put the candle back in the center and return to your place.

Priest. You are a priest or priestess. Go to a sacred place and lead or take part in a ceremony.

Some of the richest fantasy structures are those you discover for yourself. The ones above were all discovered by someone and found later to have meaning to a lot of people.

A suggested structure may not sound like much until you try it. These are often the best. If you choose one that seems off the track or confuses you, it may work better for you. If you decide in advance what a fantasy will do, what will happen, any message will have great difficulty getting through.

Your experience will never be exactly the same as another person's (3). The same triggering devices will stimulate different reactions in you on different days. In the beginning choose a fantasy and agree to do the same one for several days. This will give you a sense of how each of these tools will work for you. Fantasy structures are like a set of fine chisels. In the beginning you need only a few. As your skill develops, you reach out for more tools.

IV

Dreams

4

My DREAMS ARE uninvited messages from deep within my being. There are many ways in which I can avoid remembering these messages, but I hear them.

In 1952, it was discovered that when a person dreams his eyes move rapidly. Observations of rapid eye movement since that time have revealed a number of facts about dreams. Last night you probably had four or five dreams. Each dream lasted between ten minutes and an hour (1). There is evidence of some inner activity during all your sleep time, and it is definite that about 20 percent of that time is spent in dreaming (2). A prematurely born infant dreams 80 percent of the time he is sleeping. A child born after the full term of pregnancy dreams 50 percent of his sleep time for the first few weeks of his life. When you were a baby you spent as much time in the dream state as in the awake state (3). Your dream life is an essential part of being you. It is also an important tool for hearing yourself.

THEORY

It is difficult to dispel the academic mystique surrounding dreams, but a knowledge of some of the foremost theories may encourage you to develop your own dream theory. Every society has been interested in dreams. There were many ancient theories that a dream was a form of communication between man and God or other powerful forces. During the last few centuries a western folk theory has grown up that a dream is simply the random opening of memory banks.

Sigmund Freud may be primarily remembered for his strong argument that a dream is not a chance happening. This was a major contribution. Now we are returning to the idea of the dream as a form of communication; a way in which we can engage in a dialogue with our inner selves.

Freud's specific dream theories are quite narrow. He sees the dream as a time for wish fulfillment, for acting out frustrations. Further, he saw most of the frustrations as sexual ones. The symbols of the dreams were examined for their sexual meaning (4).

For Alfred Adler dreams touched on many subjects other than man's sexuality. To the practical Adler a dream focused on an individual's present problems and was often a way of preparing for the next day. In addition he felt the dream always contained an expression of a person's life style—the individual methods we use in approaching life's problems and possibilities (5).

Jungian and Gestalt psychology approaches are particularly useful to people who wish to use their dreams as tools of self-exploration.

According to Carl G. Jung, dreams frequently point the way in which we could grow and develop. Through the dream, voices deep within us are brought to the surface. Our unconscious tells a story to the conscious self. Unencumbered by all the details that occupy the conscious self, the unconscious can often get a clearer view of the situation and even predict the outcome of a course of action. To Jung there were no universal meanings to symbols. Each person develops his own unique language for communication between the unconscious and the conscious self.

The story of the dream is a creative act and is to be approached as we would view a painting. "Let the dream speak," is Jung's reoccurring advice.

To Jung the dream was also part of a complex balancing process of human self-regulation. If in our conscious lives we are out of balance, then, according to Jung's compensatory principle, a balance will be supplied by the unconscious. For example, a daytime life of thinking without awareness of feelings might be balanced by dreams full of raw emotions.

There is another interesting aspect to Jung's theory. He felt that dreams frequently express basic issues that go beyond a person's specific concerns. We can take clay and make a statue. The statue is unique and different from any other statue, but it also remains clay. From time to time my dreams may convey a message from my clay, that part of me that is common to all people (6).

Gestalt psychology considers man as a total organism. His dreams are a part of that total and are an important tool for becoming more truly aware of the organism. Fritz Perls taught that every part of my dream is me. I have created the dream, therefore, I am each part. If I dream of myself and an aggressive friend, I have chosen my friend as a symbol of the aggressive part of me. I can, therefore, play or speak for each part, person, and object in the dream. My personification of the part helps me hear the dream. The object is not to interpret or analyze, but to become aware of the dream and as a result to become aware of me (7).

The preceding paragraphs contain brief descriptions of some of the most important psychological dream theories. There are many other ways of seeing the dream as a religious or educational phenomenon. Kilton Stewart publicized the remarkable role of dreams in the Senoi tribe on the Malay Peninsula. Dreams are discussed every day at breakfast. From early childhood a person is encouraged to master the negative forces presented in dreams and to act out and implement the positive forces.

> If he dreams of a new trap, the elders help him to construct it, to see if it will work. If he dreams a song or poem, the elders encourage him to express it for criticism or approval. If he dreams of a girl, he is encouraged to consummate love with her in his dreams and to court her while he is awake (8).

Through an awareness of his dreams the Senoi tribesman travels the road to maturity. Children are given instructions on what to do in future dreams. Stewart's study shows that the children's dreams did change in the direction suggested by their elders. Dreams not only are seen as a tool for personal growth, but play an important part in the development of the Senoi society. The culture accepts whatever is expressed in the dream. This amounts to a full acceptance of the individual. If I accept your dreams, I accept you as you are. I do not reject you because you are not what I think you should be. The Senoi claim to be a society completely free of violent crime or mental illness. Working with dreams is seen as a way of preventing social evils (9).

Some dreams focus on practical and technical problems having little to do with spiritual or emotional development. Elias Howe discovered in a dream where to put the eye of the needle on his sewing machine. It was a dream that led Otto Loewi to the discovery that the control of the heart beat is not by direct nerve influences but through a mediating chemical. Renés Descartes' early philosophy came together in a dream.

There is a rumor around many psychological institutions that clients dream (or remember dreams) in accordance with their therapist's dream theory. Despite the objection of those who have worked so hard to develop or understand these theories, the experiences of the Senoi and others give credence to the rumor. Students sometimes report differences in their dreams as they study different theories.

Perhaps the most useful dream theory is that contained in the Talmud, which advises: "The dream is its own interpretation."

WORKING WITH DREAMS

How do I become aware of the activities of my dream state when I am awake? How can I listen to my dreams and learn from my dreams? Let us focus on these and other practical questions.

1. *Recording.* The best way to remember a dream is to record it. Often I have only a hazy sense of the dream, but as I start to write, other parts begin to come. For this reason I sometimes begin to write in the middle of a page so that I can add what came before as it returns to me.

Dreams should be written as stories. There should be no explanations, justifications, or analysis. The more we try to explain a dream the more elusive our memory of the dream becomes.

When I am awake I am concerned with many issues that are irrelevant in my dream life, and the memory of the dream passes quickly. The best time to record a dream would be while I am dreaming, but I do not not know how to do it. There is a time when I am neither fully asleep nor fully awake. This is called the hypnopompic state, which is itself often rich in experiences. As I begin to move out of the hypnopompic state I am not yet focusing on the concerns of my awake life and I am able to write. This is the best time to begin to record a dream.

Dreams recorded at this time may be incomplete and in very poor writing, but you have secured a piece of the dream and you can use that piece to later reconstruct the dream. The act of recording the dream helps me keep the experience alive in my awake state. When I return to the page it helps me return to the emotional state I experienced while recording the dream.

It is not necessary that you remember the whole dream. Perhaps no one has ever been completely aware of a dream. You can work with a fragment of a dream. If you keep your journal within reach of the bed you eliminate another excuse for forgetting the dream.

Do not start to analyze the dream. Become aware of the dream. Let the story of the dream speak to you for a few hours or a few days. When you really hear the story, then is the time to begin to work at learning from the dream.

2. *Preludes and Series.* Sometimes there is a strong sense of two dreams going together. They may seem like two parts of the same experience, yet the content is very different. Often the first dream is a guide to what to look for in the second. The first dream is the prelude; it contains the moral. "The main message in the dream you are about to see concerns the following issue . . ."

Dreams are often in series. Dream after dream will relate to the same issues. The content will change but the message will remain the same. Then suddenly this will change. Frequently, this occurs after having begun to work with a particular dream or a series. As the gap between the dream state and the waking state closes, the activities in the dream state often appear to shift.

3. *Speaking for a Part.* Gestalt psychology gives us a helpful suggestion. I can become any person or object in my dream. My voice can be the medium for the part. Since I selected the symbol to have a particular meaning in my dream, it is possible to reverse the process and to move from the symbol to the meaning. As I play the part, I very likely move out of the dream. My conscious mind may insist that a dream about a field of strawberries is a symbol of inner tranquility. Yet when I become a strawberry I may feel and say, "I am small and helpless, I cannot move, I must lie here in danger of being stepped on."

Speaking for one or several parts of a dream enable me to quickly break through a pseudounderstanding into an awareness of the dream.

4. *Working with Other People.* Others who are also working with dreams can be helpful in gaining an awareness of your own dream. However, there is a danger. The chances are that you already automatically analyze the dream too much. You do not need more analysis. You do not need anyone to tell you what your dreams mean. The following are some guidelines in working with other people:

[a] Work only with people who are also collecting dreams.

[b] Tell your dream as you would tell a story. Do not add explanations or comments before, during, or afterward.

[c] The people to whom you are telling your dream should close their eyes and experience the dream. Your dream becomes their fantasy.

[d] They tell you what happened to them as they experienced the dream. What is shared are feelings, not thoughts, and these feelings are not always easy to bring out. The first statements may be cryptic. "I feel sad." "I am angry." As the exchange of feeling takes place, it becomes easier for a person to express his experience.

[e] The other people are talking about their experiences, not your dream. It is up to you to get what you need from what is being shared with you. You will begin to have strong reactions as you hear other people speak or as you speak for a part. You will be hit by the rightness of some things, and others will go past you. This awareness is sometimes almost a physical reaction.

[f] Do not argue about interpretations or get involved with irrelevant matters. I am not interested in what you think my experience should mean to me; I want to know what it means to you. Do not let anyone judge the dream. Even positive judgments like "Wow, what a great dream!" can cloud an awareness of the dream.

[g] Sometimes the other people will have difficulty in getting involved with your dream. At these times they can ask you to repeat the dream. On rare occasions they can ask you to speak for a part. But this is more appropriately a suggestion you make to yourself and should never be a substitute for a person's own investment in the dream. How-

ever, at times this is a method for getting involved in the dream when nothing else works.

[h] Each person must take responsibility for himself. No one should try to be a helper. If you feel you are talking to the dreamer when you are sharing your reactions, you are probably giving an analysis rather than your own emotions.

5. *Clues.* Often an awareness of the dream will enrich my life. At other times some action is suggested. These are the "clues" in the dream.

A suggestion is not viable until I have a genuine awareness of the dream. "I hear what the dream is saying; now what do I do about it?" probably means, "I am not fully aware of the dream. I do not really hear what it is saying." After I have experienced the story of the dream, clues will frequently appear. I have the sense that dreams are often the classes of the teacher within, and he has no intention of making his suggestions until I am ready to hear them. Working on a dream can help me become aware of an earlier dream. Weeks or months later I can return to a dream and find the clue, by now quite obvious. "I am taking an indirect path." "I am denying my feelings." These become specific suggestions for changes in my life.

Sometimes there is a resolution in the dream. A problem in my waking life is taken into the dream state and resolved. In myself these healing resolutions have usually focused on deficiencies: overcoming a depression, getting rid of generalized anxiety. The refreshed sensation is like having an aching tooth fixed while you were asleep.

6. *Humor.* The heavy and melodramatic nature of many dreams often turns out to be a way of laughing at ourselves for taking ourselves too seriously. Other people can help us

see the humor in our dreams. If I am choosing to view something as a very heavy situation, my dream may push the situation to an extreme, but it seems logical to me. It takes someone's laughter to burst the melodramatic bubble.

There are frequently puns in dreams (10). There can be a play on words or acting out of a cliché. These may be sources of embarrassment to our sophisticated conscious selves. Sometimes the pun is elaborate. A friend had a dream in which he was bound with rope and stuck on the ceiling as his new boss came into the room. Someone hearing the dream suggested it contained a pun on being "uptight." My friend had previously denied any such reaction to his new boss. After the dream he allowed himself to become aware of his uneasiness and worked it through.

7. *Symbols and Signs.* Jung makes a distinction between symbols and signs. A sign is less than what it represents. A sign pointing the direction to a city is less than the city. A symbol stands for something more than is obvious. A great dragon breathing fire can be a symbol of my anger. A sign is always linked to the conscious thought behind it, whereas symbols are natural and spontaneous events. No one ever invented a symbol.

There is no universal meaning to symbols. You and I could have the same symbols and they would mean very different things in each of our dreams. The color black can be warm and protective to you and frightening to me. I can experience your dream not because of a knowledge of your symbols, but because I become involved with how the symbols are put together—in other words, the story of the dream. Neither you nor I can hear the story if either of us insists on seeing a symbol only in a preconceived fashion.

8. *Drugs.* There is evidence that chemical agents reduce the amount of dream time in periods of sleep. This is particularly true with alcohol, amphetamines, and barbiturates. When a person stops using the agent, there are often vivid dream and quasi-dream experiences. It has been suggested that this is an attempt of the dream state to catch up. Some research is going into developing drugs that do not interfere with dreams, but at present chemical agents can make the communication between the dream state and awake state more difficult. Preliminary studies at UCLA Medical Center suggest that heavy smokers seldom achieve deep sleep and have fewer than normal dreams. Not only does reducing the number of dreams interfere with self-exploration, but also it can contribute to a general nervous and anxious condition and other emotional pain (11).

9. *Borderline States.* The hynogogic state occurs between waking and going to sleep. The hypnopompic state is between sleeping and waking up. There are often very rich experiences that occur in these states that can be used as tools of self-exploration in the same way you work with a dream from a deep sleep (12).

THE DREAM EXPERIENCE

The following are a number of dreams that have been borrowed from several friends. The dreams are followed by my own fantasies. Your fantasy could be quite different from mine. The person who dreamed it could also hear something quite different. There is much more to the story of each of these dreams than we can explore here.

Remember that with your dreams and the dreams of

others, the object is not to control and nail down the inner world, but to learn to live there (13).

There are different emphases in dreams. When there are many games in our conscious lives, our dreams are often painfully honest about what is really going on with us. Then again there may be dramatic, selfless dreams in which we transcend our individual concerns and travel into an almost archetypal portion of our inner space. The dreams shared here are of a practical nature. These dreams were helpful to the people involved in taking a next step toward a more nourishing life. These are typical of the kinds of experiences in the first year or so of seriously collecting and listening to dreams.

Before you read the following dreams, write down one of your dreams. It does not have to be complete or recent. As you read the dreams that follow, try to become part of each one. Take a minute after reading the story of the dream and experience it yourself before reading my comments.

Andrew's Dream

I am in a temple for the Holy Days. There is an obnoxious man leading the services. My friend and I leave. I work hard to get out, I push through the many people on the steps. I realize I left my overcoat. I call to Rona to wait. I must return. I squeeze up through the four-floor shaft. It is tight and difficult to breathe. I arrive. A man is persisting in his craziness. I am alone with him at the top of the building. We struggle. I kill this person. I believe I throw him off the building. I have a long knife slash on my left arm. The elevator goes down to pick up Rona. I feel weak, my shirt is off. I'm waiting for Rona. We embrace. I see the concern in her face. I back away.

My Fantasy. *I'm moving. I'm leaving. I'm in a new place. I don't want to go back, but I must have my coat. I don't need my coat, but I've got to have my coat. I hate it. I'm out. I'm more vulnerable. I'm naked. I'm hurt. Don't look at me. If you see I'm hurt, if you see I'm defective, you'll go away and leave me.*

My Comment. Andrew was a brilliant young physician just beginning his psychiatric residency. Through a rigorous school career he had moved efficiently and at high speed. He came to the Humanist Institute as a way of gaining more skill for his professional work. In the course of his experiences he opened the door on the warm and feeling side of his personality.

This is what Andrew heard when working with his own dream:

"*The services are the old way, the obnoxious way. I can get away. To hell with the old ways. It's work and I can do it. I've left my overcoat, my shell, my covering. Damn the coat, I can leave the coat, I don't need the coat. I need my coat, my shell. I'm suffocating—I can't breathe—my energy is stopped. I hold myself in. I won't let myself go. I won't give up the old ways.*

"*I'm crazy—you're crazy—this is crazy. I'm losing my mind, I'm losing control. I'm scared, I'm out of control, stop me! Stop him! Stop this craziness. Kill him—kill me.*

"*I'm alone—I can win. I can destroy the madness. I'm powerful, I'm victorious.*

"*I'm hurt, I'm vulnerable, my left arm is vulnerable. I'm shirtless, I'm exposed, I'm naked. My right arm is strong; invulnerable.*

"We embrace—I see concern. If you see a weakness you'll go. You won't accept a weakness. You won't accept me. I won't accept my weakness. I won't accept me."

Martha's Dream

I am working at a border where two warring countries meet. There is a friendly rivalry between the guards on each side. There is a door with a glass in the top through the wall—it never seems to be locked. Somehow one of the enemy loses his head on my side of the wall. It is lying under some clear water near the wall. I had something to do with his death.

Someone comes through the door to my side—he is escaping and being chased. I lean against the door to delay his pursuers. He runs out to the road and soldiers start helping him into a truck. His pursuer gets through the door and starts shooting at him. I begin to make love to the pursuer to distract him. We playfully roll around on the ground and tease each other. Finally we come to rest and he looks up and sees the head near-by. It reminds him that we are enemies and he stalks off.

Some men from my side come along and one talks to me while the others play cards near the wall. I show him the head. He picks it up and puts it on over his own head. We then walk toward the other people to show them. They don't notice that he is wearing someone else's head. He takes it off and there is blood on his gray sweat shirt hood. We all tell him his trip will be ruined because there is blood on his sweat shirt. He says, "No, it is of no importance."

My Fantasy. I feel trapped, I feel dull, I am in a fight. There are good guys and bad guys. They are roles, I am a role. Nothing personal passes between us. Changing heads or roles

*does not make any difference. Also, I act as if I had nothing
to do with cutting off the head. I want to move out of this
war game completely.*

My Comment. On one level this dream related to
Martha's handling a specific, complicated, and difficult work
problem. The dream was like a warning light that the ad-
ministrative part of her was reaching the maximum allow-
able percentage of her total personality. Months later she
also heard a clue on another level about the importance of
accepting her own head and being more centered in her
own life.

David's Dream

*I see an eaglelike bird, all black. The bird picks me up and
carries me upwards. I hear these words: BY LIFTING YOU
UP I WILL FREE YOU FROM ALL THESE THINGS.*

My Fantasy. *I am new, awed, centered. I feel shaken up
and different. I feel as if there is no past.*

My Comment. David was a member of a religious order.
He was being considered for the position of Superior of his
community. He was worried. How could he detach from all
the nice things of life that he liked: art, books, academic
achievements. How could he do all that was necessary to be
a good Superior. He was stunned and helped by this potent
dream. It was like a slap in the face telling him to quit
fooling around with all his little worries. The path of a
Superior could be a way of transcending his former vision
of life. David accepted the position and has found it a nourishing spiritual path. He has brought much richness to his
community. Sometime later David said that the dream

showed that "I will be purified in my spiritual path toward God through my office as Superior. It will teach me an approach to detachment or a way to it that I may not have chosen myself" (14).

William's Dream

I am in an operating room with several other doctors. I donate the left lens of my glasses. A doctor takes it out and puts it into another doctor's glasses. The doctor who owns the glasses is drunk and uncooperative. He is rubbing his eyes. I have a feeling that the glasses are not for the doctor. Then I realize I am without a lens. I ask about the consequences to me—not seeing well, glare, etc. I get angry and consider malpractice. They apologize and try to get me another lens.

My Fantasy. I don't feel an equal here. I will volunteer my lens to buy acceptance. Now I'm angry. I'm out of focus, I can't see. It's someone else's fault. I'm not going to let this go on. Get me back my lens or I'll tell! I feel like a character in a Charlie Chaplin movie. I want out before anything else goes wrong.

My Comment. William found a valuable clue about the wasted energy in his games for recognition. The feelings and thoughts he had in reading this dream several weeks later were:

"I feel naive, as if I have been used. I feel guilty. I should not have let them have the lens. I feel out of control and helpless. I get angry. When I consider malpractice, I feel strong and that I am in control.

"The clue for me is to be more in touch with what I want, and what I can do, without leaning on others. I gave the

lens to make 'them' notice me. I'll get it back by having
the authorities (another 'them') force them to give it back."

Matthew's Dream

I am in a sacred place. I am here for a vigil. It is a long
night. I feel purified and waiting. As dawn begins to break
several people come near me. I recognize them. They are all
ordinary people I know. Yet they look different. I can see the
spirituality in each of them. I feel humble and strong. Each
one slowly approaches me, looks into my eyes, and says something to me. Then the person steps back. This is what they
each said. "Love—there are no excuses!" "Be simple." "BE
STRONG!" "Teach by sharing you and receiving me." "Hold
without smothering." "Listen." "Accept." "Stop—open your
eyes—be." "Be practical." "Come together." "Play."

Now the sky is red and gold with dawn. I realize that I am
in the center of a circle. I kneel. It is very still. Each person
comes and puts his hands on my head and then I rise. We all
smile. Arm in arm we walk off toward a large group of happy
people.

My Fantasy. I am pure, clean, new. This feels like an ordi-
nation. I can really see people. I am being myself. There are
no games. I feel at home and peaceful.

My Comment. Matthew is trained in a very competitive
profession. Some years back he became an administrator of
a nonprofit group. This brought him closer to people, but he
was still involved in a lot of business affairs. Then he took
a risk and joined with some people who wanted to build a
center for their own growth. Matthew was being looked at
as a leader, but he was still hesitant about trusting his insights and intuitions. He took a lot of half steps. The group

had come together for a weekend in order to solve a number of little problems. The first day was filled with a lot of dulling discussions, none of which seemed really relevant. That night Matthew had his dream. It filled him up. On the next morning he shared the dream. The people were struck by it. The people at the meeting were in the dream. All the petty things dropped away. That day the group moved with bold steps to actualize their dreams. Several years later Matthew said, "I was afraid to be myself. In the dream I saw who I was. Dreams are still helping me become me."

Mary's Dream

I am walking with my cat. Only now the cat is a young girl. I say that she can come to a party that I am going to, if she doesn't turn back into a cat. She says that she would not do that. We go in. We talk about the vegetables we are growing in the field beside a big house. We only planted them yesterday and they are ready. We will use them to make a salad for the party. I go into the big house and sit in a booth with several other people. Some old men are sitting behind us. They send a young boy who asks me if one old man can say I requested a particular song when he gets up to play his fiddle. I say "yes." The old man smiles at me. Swan Lake begins to play and people stand up and begin to move. I think at first that they all know particular movements that they are doing together. Then I see that they are doing whatever they want to. I step out of the booth so that I will have more room. I take off my shoes. I start to worry about how I will make preparations for dinner with everyone already there. I look down to the end of the room where the ovens are and see that all the counterspace around them is taken up with people. I wonder how I can make the cookies. I go toward the front

of the building looking for my friend the cat. I do not see her.
I go outside and she is there. I say we must go get some yogurt
for the gravy and then go out into the field and pick the vegetables. She says yogurt is available on the fourth floor of this
building. We do not have to go to the store. I hesitate and
then decide this is a good idea. She says she will get the yogurt
and meet me in the field.

(There is a shift)

She has given me the yogurt and I put cranberry sauce in it.
I realize that has ruined it for the gravy. I decide to go back up
to the fourth floor for more. When I get there, it is the film
department. A man is coming out of the door with a movie
camera on his shoulder. He says we can use it for the event
today. I am very appreciative. I remember we need some yogurt
and I tell him. He goes back in the door and out a side way.
I follow. He calls back that to get the yogurt we have to go
the poison oak way. He is jumping down a path that I can
see is overgrown with poison oak. I don't know if I am supposed to follow him. I begin jumping from one clean spot to
another. I am moving very fast sailing through the air long
distances. We are in a field with many paths. The cat girl is
here now too. We take a turn and the path is very muddy. We
sink up over our knees. This seems to be a wider main path.
I am certain that it is the most direct one. The side paths all
seem to be muddy too. I keep going. I am not very bothered
by the mud. I think it will make my legs look tan.

My Fantasy. In the beginning, I am polite. I am doing
what other people want me to. I don't want the cat to embarrass me. I want her to accommodate. I am doing something
I know is wrong. I don't want yogurt and gravy together. I
appreciate the man. I want him to give me more directions.
I don't know what to do. I am feeling lost. Now I feel good.

*I feel moving out, jumping. I am listening to me. I am doing
the right thing. I am on the right path. I feel vital.*

My Comment. Mary was a remarkable person whose
gifts were locked up in her polite and accommodating nature.
This dream came to her at a time when she had withdrawn
for a few days in order to find a way of liberating the new
strength she was feeling within her. To her there was a
practical message in the dream that she should accommodate
less and trust in herself more. The feelings she experienced
in the dream were extremely intense. She wanted to relive
jumping down the path in her conscious life. Her feelings
about the dream were these:

*I feel as if I am on the right path and I am going to keep on
this one even though it is muddy. All the other paths are
muddy too! In the beginning of the dream I felt disorganized
and hassled, not ready or prepared. When I focused on the
cat-girl I felt centered. I felt as if she knew what was important;
that she was quiet and could not be pulled off the path. I felt
as if I was too worried about whether the cat-girl was going to
embarrass me. I want to be more like her; more free, more . . .
just myself.*

My Dream

*I am at an army base. Barracks are facing a railroad track.
I am behind the barracks. The barracks are between me and
the tracks. A troop train starts by. It becomes a very elaborate
display. There are tall men standing on flatbeds, holding huge
flags which flow dramatically. "One general showing off to
another," suggests someone near me. A man dressed in frogman gear gets off the train and moves by floating through the*

air and begins spraying paint on the back side of the barracks. The frogman and the impressive train move parallel. "What is this," someone asks, "one general playing a joke on another?"

The dream shifts to a quiet city street. The frogman is without his suit. He is smiling and confident. Two men jump him. He easily subdues them. Another man who was on the troop train comes and humbly approaches the frogman with respect and admiration. They wrestle. The frogman wins. They both laugh. They wrestle more and the fight evolves into a joyful dance.

My Comment. This is my dream. The man who gets things done, the control man, the impressor, does his thing well, right down the track. The playful man, the poet, also does his thing. These two parts are in me. They are both me. They are in competition. One must win and the other must lose. In this dream these two meet head on for the first time. They fight with each other and find that they are two forces that can complement each other. Such a possibility had never occurred to me in or out of a dream! Months later I recognized the frogman as a relative to the toad in Issa's haiku (see page 12). Then I also heard a clue to find enrichment in simple things.

Your Dream

Now read your dream and listen to the story.

V

Art Experiences

EVERYONE IS AN artist. That includes you. There are many expressions of artistic ability. You can develop your talent, study your art, and create things aesthetically pleasing to you and others. But here we will explore art as a tool of self-exploration. We are not concerned with the aesthetic experience. Although, if you do not have any a priori conceptions, then your work will be bona fide art and therefore —aesthetical. When you are natural you are genuine.

The artist in you lives at the center. If the conscious self can be distracted, your body can become the medium for expressing a message from the self in a concrete form that can be seen with your eyes and felt with your hands.

ART AND GROWTH

Art experiences are being recognized as important tools for all areas of human growth. Until recent years, working with art materials was seen only as an opportunity to express creativity or work out frustrations. Now, we recognize that art is itself an experience, something artists have always known.

You can increase awareness of your problems with art, overcome interpersonal difficulties, test your honesty and spontaneity, or help build a group. Art is useful anywhere there is a desire for growth (1).

The message from the self to my conscious being can be in the preverbal language of art. In order to allow the message to come, it is important to let things happen; not to plan or create anything. There is no place for aesthetic judgments or aspirations. How it looks is irrelevant. It does not have to please anyone. It is a message.

THE ART EXPERIENCE

The following are a few specific suggestions on the use of art materials. Many others will occur to you as you begin using this tool.

PAPER

Choose two sheets of white paper. Use good-sized sheets, at least 12" x 18" in size. Get a box of oil pastels. Take the paper labels off the pastels. Other media can be used, such as chalk, crayons, or felt pens. However, in the beginning pastels are best. Watercolors, poster paints, oil paints, and acrylics are too complex in preparation and application unless you are trained in their use.

Get the materials now and take part in the experience as you are reading the instructions below.

Take the two sheets of paper and the box of pastels. Place the paper on a firm, hard surface. Push one sheet of paper to one side. Choose one color. Pick it up. Close your eyes and make simple movements in the air. Make circles, crosses, curves, straight lines, and whatever other motions occur to you. One motion will begin to feel more right or intense than another. When this occurs, open your eyes and put your motion on the paper. Repeat the motion over and over. Begin to exaggerate the motion. Make a sound to go with the motion. When you are finished become passive and look at the paper. If you are working with other people, share your experience by making your motion and your sound. Do not say anything else.

Put a clean sheet of paper in front of you. Experience the paper. Focus on the paper. Look at it. Feel it. While looking at the paper, say to yourself several times, "This is me. This is me." Do not plan anything. Look at the paper until you want to put something on the paper. Using whatever colors you wish, make whatever feels right. When you are finished, again say to yourself, "This is me." Become passive. Look at and listen to the paper. If others are with you, introduce yourself with the paper. Speak for the picture. Speak in the first person. Start by saying, "This is me. I am _____." Do not describe the painting or analyze it. Do not edit or control what comes. Do not plan what you are going to say.

CLAY

Purchase twenty-five pounds of inexpensive quarry tile clay and get a wooden or masonite board about 15″ x 15″. Keep the clay in a container with a moist rag on top. Whenever you use it and return it to the container, push the clay together. If the clay gets dry, push several small but deep holes into the clay and pour in a little water, and work the clay.

Get down on the floor with the board and clay near you. Take a minute to become quiet. Reach into the container and experiment with the amount of clay that feels right in your hands. Feel the weight and begin to work the clay. Do not construct anything. Experience the clay's hardness and its malleability.

Close your eyes and play with the clay. Do to the clay what you want for yourself. If you want to be stroked, pet the clay. If you want to feel firmer at this moment, make the clay firm. In this manner, let your hands move. Push the clay around.

A shape will begin to form. Usually it is an abstract shape. Let your hands decide what feels right. Open your eyes after the shape has begun to form. If you sense yourself constructing or controlling what you are doing, close your eyes again. All the time your hands are moving. Stop when your hands begin to slow down. Remain quiet for a brief moment. Look at the clay. Close your eyes and pick up or put your hands on the clay. Say to yourself, "This is me." Be still.

If other people are also using clay, introduce yourself to the group with the clay. Speak for the clay. Then start moving your hands again and speak for your hands; say what your hands are doing.

DOODLES

Doodles done every day can also be a way of listening to ourselves. Put a pencil on the page and doodle. Some prefer to look away and scratch out motions for a few seconds. Often these scribbles do not say much to us until we have collected about half a dozen or so. Some people do not look at what they have drawn until the next day.

MANDALAS

A mandala is a circular drawing used as an aid for focusing in some schools of meditation (2). It is seen by some as a magic circle. Carl G. Jung used it as a symbol of the self and saw it as an assistance in producing a new center of personality.

During the year Jung spent as a medical officer in World War I, he drew a mandala each day. He found that these

". . . seemed to correspond to my [his] inner situation at the time. . . ."

> My mandalas were cryptograms concerning the state of the self which was presented to me anew each day. In them I saw the self—that is, my whole being—actively at work (3).

Commit yourself to draw a mandala each day for a month. It can be anything so long as there is a center to the drawing. Have a variety of colored pens or pastels at your disposal. Do not plan anything. Simply begin to draw.

As Jung discovered, this exercise does more than give insight. It can itself be a ". . . path to the center" (4).

COLLECTING THE PIECES

For most of us the art experience tells what is most immediate in our inner world. If we agree to work with paper for a month, at the end of that time we have many pieces of the picture. The same thing can be done with clay, but the collecting gets cumbersome. When we have a number of these pictures, we can hear not only what is there but also what is not there.

Working with a number of pictures can be enriching. Spread your pictures on the floor. Do not say anything. Let a friend move the pictures around without comment. He can play with any patterns he sees between pictures. It makes no difference what he does so long as he moves them. Be aware of your own reactions. When he stops, you begin moving the pictures around. When they are where you want them, quickly speak for each picture. It sometimes helps to

look at each paper and say, "I am aware of _____,"
and move on to the next picture. At the end, accept all
the pictures as pieces of you and begin to describe yourself by looking at all the pictures once more and saying, "I
am _____."

One of my colleagues at the Humanist Institute kept a
doodle diary. He has no special artistic skills. Each day he
simply played on a sheet of paper and then put it aside.
He kept this up for three weeks. At the end of that time
he followed the foregoing suggestions. After a friend rear-
ranged the pictures, he looked at each one and verbalized
his strongest feelings and perceptions at that moment. These
were all preceded with the phrase "I'm aware of _____."
Usually he began the phrase with no sense of what would
follow.

When finished, he looked at each picture again and said,
"I am _____."

These two comments are below each picture in the following pages.

1

I am aware of darkness, sharpness, boldness.

—

I am sharp.

2

I am aware of parts, eye, spiral.
—
I am not together.

3
I am aware of three centers of movement.
—
I am separated.

4
I am aware of sharpness, of closing.

—

I am afraid.

5

I am aware of power, thunder and lightning!

—

I am powerful!

6

I am aware of being surrounded, of giving off bubbles.
—
I am giving.

7

I am aware of a head, breast, hair, box.
—
I am mysterious.

8

I am aware of a monkey.
—
I am childlike.

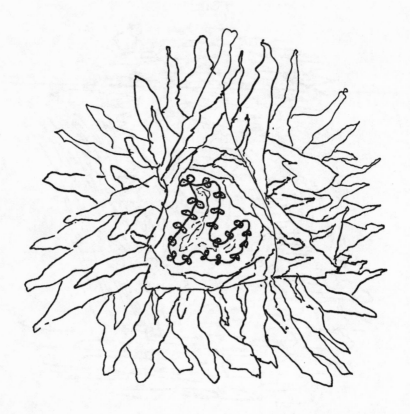

9

I am aware of a center, of harshness.

—

I am dangerous.

10

I am aware of a fireball, of flames going out.
—
I am fiery.

11
I am aware of a cloud, of being contained.

—

I am lonely.

12

I am aware of black dots, of not pulling together.

—

I am enclosed.

13

I am aware of separation, of no connection, unconcerned, uneasy, sin.

—

I am vicious.

14

I am aware of an animal, of coming out, of gayness, of exploding.
—
I am growing.

15
I am aware of a spring, a tree.
—
I am stable.

16

I am aware of the center, being together.

—

I am contented.

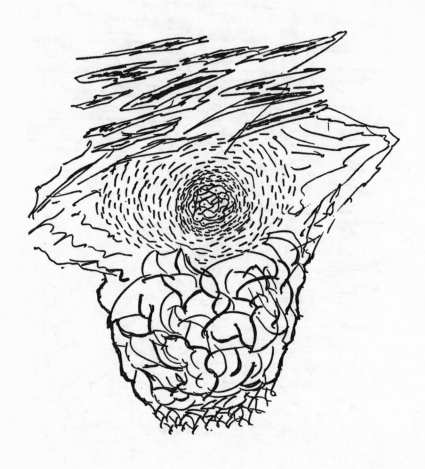

17
I am aware of grounding, of topheaviness, of the center.
—
I am centered.

18
I am aware of playfulness, of simplicity.
—
I am playful.

19
I am aware of a sailboat, of smallness, of flowing.
—
I am graceful.

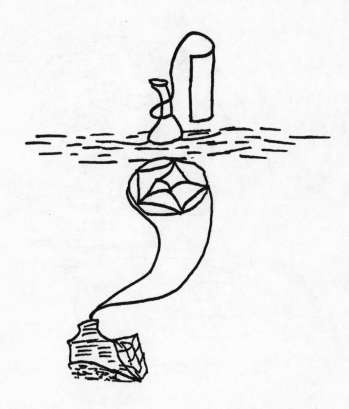

20

I am aware of an outward motion, of separateness.

—

I am disconnected.

21
I am aware of pieces, of fear.
—
I am mysterious.

After he finished, I asked my friend to construct a picture of himself using the words in the "I am" sentences. He said:

I am a person who often feels separated, disconnected, not together. I am powerful, fiery, sharp, and graceful, and at times I feel afraid, mysterious, and even vicious and dangerous. I am giving, and I am enclosed. I am childlike and playful. I am stable. I am contented. I am growing. I am centered.

When asked what was not in his profile that he would like there, he responded quickly:

I want to be warmer. I want to be more accepting.

What he said he was and what he wanted sounded very authentic to my friend and those of us in the room. It was one of those rare moments when nothing is missing.

"You must treat a work of art like a great man," advises Arthur Schopenhauer (5). "Stand before it and wait patiently until it deigns to speak." What you do is a work of art. Stand before it.

VI

Meditation

MEDITATION IS A good and simple thing. But most people see it as a complex, specialized, and mysterious process. A toad meditates all the time. The toad is not trying to achieve any high state. He is just being himself. So you can begin to meditate by imitating the toad.

This chapter is not a treatise on meditation, but an attempt to be of practical assistance to those who wish to incorporate the practice of meditation into their everyday lives.

Before considering specific personal methods of meditation, let us start with an overall exploration of the whole concept in order to dispel any feeling that it is a practice only for the spiritually elite.

DEFINITIONS AND FUNCTIONS

All religious systems have been concerned with communication. In the West, the form of communication has usually been speaking and is embodied in the concept of prayer. In the East, religious communication has focused on the process of listening. Meditation evolved into one of the most important ways of listening.

The definition and practice of meditation is seldom the same for any two people. Meditative practices are often linked with definite systems of belief. These systems often have a particular idea about reality or growth, and meditation is seen as a way of experiencing those concepts.

However, meditation does not have to be connected with a particular belief system. There are general forms of meditation which are good for their own sake.

TECHNIQUES OF MEDITATION

There are thousands of meditative techniques. Any particular technique would emphasize the attitudes of the particular religious or philosophical group in which it developed. Many meditative practices would have relevance only to certain groups; for example, there are some Buddhists who meditate on the body by becoming absorbed in the concept of dead, decaying bodies. This technique is used as a discipline to develop a distaste for our body and to give up the restriction of feeling proud of our special body and therefore possessed by it. In this fashion the Buddhist can move closer to the concept of the universal. Other religions not having this particular view of what it means to grow would not encourage such a meditation.

The meditative practices of Mahayana Buddhism can be seen in seven groups, many of which have application in learning to listen to the world of me.

1. *Breathing Exercises.* This practice is explored later.

2. *Focusing on a Point.* By focusing on a particular point or object, such as a candle flame, a rock, or flower petal, you gradually learn to get outside your mental set. One of the Chinese words for meditation means the "union of me and the object," not as a conqueror but as a peer. I do not control the object or clinically observe the object, but I join with the object.

Another approach to this type of meditation is focusing upon points that you cannot see. For example, focusing on a point between your eyebrows, on your heart center, on your navel, or on space.

3. *Sounds.* Although the use of sounds, such as vocal

prayers or mantras, is more common to Hindu approaches, it was used by many Buddhists. One was not necessarily praying to any one thing or person. For example, there are forms of meditation that consist of repeating a simple sound a thousand or million times. "OM" is a mantra that for those who use it often has all meaning and no meaning at the same time. A mantra is constantly repeated in order to achieve a great sense of unity with all that is around us. There are forms of meditation that consist of listening to the sound of your breath and gradually liberating the sounds you feel in your throat and body.

4. *Visualization.* This form of meditation is a long process. It consists of visualizing something very specific, such as a Buddha sitting on your head. An individual would engage in this practice for many years. A variation is to close your eyes and imagine a spot several feet in front of you. Visualize you sitting there.

5. *Movement.* Many individual Buddhists have followed the ancient forms of meditation through movement, such as the Chinese Tai Chi (1), which allows us, through a series of exercises, to have a greater sense of the forces within our bodies and to bring these forces into harmony. Movement as meditation or as preparation to meditate plays an important role in the various systems of Yoga (2).

The use of movement in religious practices is at times seen as a danger by the predominant society. The Sufi dances of the Near East were outlawed largely out of fear that they would liberate the basic passion in men. From the beginning of the Western witchcraft cults in the fifteenth century, movement of some sort played important roles in their rituals. One of these exercises was known as the Widdershin. A variation on the Widdershin is a simple and effective means of meditation and consists simply of standing in a relaxed position with the hands extended straight out and beginning to turn slowly in a counterclockwise movement and turning faster, always going a little bit faster than seems comfortable. As a person surrenders control over his mental faculties, his ability to stay up increases. At some point you stop and act upon whatever message you receive from your body. Remaining quiet in that position for a few moments is a means of basic communication with the total organism of the self.

6. *Devotional Practices.* A person can focus upon various thoughts or texts. This is a passive meditation, not an active mental reflection or concentration. You put the thought or text before you as if you were focusing on an object. An example of this is the Zen *koans*, which often consist of questions that cannot be answered by the logical mind. Another approach is to focus on the "four unlimited thoughts" found in many schools of Buddhism, which are friendliness, compassion, sympathetic joy, evenmindedness. This type of meditation emphasizes the connections between all people.

7. *Meditation Without Method.* In this form you do not meditate by using any of the other methods. Here there is no system, no focusing on the particular object, no use of sound, movement, or text. It is sometimes referred to as the effortless meditation—entering the "gateless gate." Meditation becomes a necessary part of life and a natural and spontaneous event.

PASSIVITY

Those schools of Buddhism that advocate practices similar to the ones outlined above frequently speak of three stages of meditation. The first stage of meditation is filled with disruptions that seem to increase, but this is not the case. Through meditation, you become aware of how many distracting thoughts you have in your mind. This step is not to be avoided or controlled, because the attempt to control the distraction becomes another distraction.

In the second step, the distracting thoughts intrude less. You then begin to sense sounds, visions, and odors, and to become involved with many mental images and activities. These are to be avoided. Here is perhaps one reason for Carl G. Jung's reservation about meditation as a practice for westerners. It was his belief that these images can tell us a great deal about ourselves. This is definitely true; fantasies and dreams are equally important and legitimate approaches to discovering the world of me, but these approaches are separate, and each method requires its own discipline. Visions can become so strong that they stop the meditative process.

The third stage allows you to hear yourself in your own language, and allows you to discover alternatives for further steps. To the Buddhists, it is the beginning of the road to becoming a Buddha. But this road does not go anywhere. You do not meditate for enlightenment. When you meditate, you are enlightened. Meditation is simply a way of being yourself. The road keeps going back to where you have already been.

The initial exercises in any meditative practice are an

attempt to clear the mind, to help us slow down. Often I am not able to turn off my busy preoccupations, and it is in these times that it is helpful to be able to use exercises that require not less, but greater, concentration. I intensify my distracting tendency, but in an area that will lead me into a meditative attitude. If my mind is racing, I can treat it like a child and instead of insisting that it be quiet, distract it by giving it something else to be busy with, and insist that it become even busier. This is partly what happens in the breathing exercises that are discussed later. It can be done with such simple things as focusing on the concept of black; focusing very hard, using my whole body to help the focus, then releasing the tension in my body and inside of me, and then again focusing and again releasing the tension.

Passivity is the key to meditation. This is a simple but essential statement that needs to be frequently restated. Meditation is a deep passivity combined with awareness. It is a suspension of thinking and other busy activities. I become passive, even to my own thoughts and problems, and give up those strong habits of trying to control a situation. When I am in control of me, then I do not hear me. Of course it is a risk to be passive, but when I take that risk I can listen.

"Meditation" is a European word that does not very accurately describe the process. Both "meditation" and "medical" come from the same Latin word for "measure." One is the measure of man's injuries and ills, and the other a mental measuring of an idea or fact. From this comes a connotation of active, studied, thinking, grasping, comprehending. The Tibetan word for meditation is a much more accurate connotation of the process. It means the stabilized mind, which gives at the same time the image of passiveness and awareness.

A MANY-PETALED FLOWER

The many approaches to meditation can be confusing. Out of this confusion meditation fads arise. The schools of meditation are not so much competing cults as petals of the same flower. All the disciplines agree that the thinking, cognitive mind must yield to other ways of being and experiencing. How to achieve this is the point of departure. Japan was a very crowded country and life was a continual distraction, and so Japanese meditation methods emphasize training in learning to have a single focus. China was an agrarian society and its meditative experiences emphasize the changes within us. In nature, spring implies autumn. In me, sorrow implies joy. Through meditation I learn to flow. The phenomenal world in India was filled with misery. The Indian meditation methods are spirituals highs, ways of living someplace else.

For most of us, the environment is similar to that which existed in Japan. So I find focusing exercises most helpful, and this is reflected in what follows. But there are times when I am nearer to classical China or even ancient India.

There are also western petals on this flower. The medieval mystics called meditation the "Prayer of Quiet" or the "Prayer of the Heart." A number of eastern Christians followed the Hesychast approach and tried to live up to St. Paul's admonition to pray without ceasing (3). The main method was the "Jesus Prayer," which was common throughout the Near East, Greece, and Russia. The practice still continues there and has recently begun to attract attention in western Christian circles. Although there are many formulas, one of the most common practices was to say constantly "Lord Jesus Christ have mercy on me a sinner." After a person was well on the way to reciting this prayer with every breath, he would then begin to focus on his heart. Some words of the prayer would become associated with the automatic movements of the heart or lungs. Then the process became less a matter of will and more a peaceful resting in a spiritual life. A modern writer on western mysticism describes the Prayer of Quiet as one in which the "self is content to rest in a new level of vivid awareness, marked by a deep peace and living stillness" (4).

Gradually this western mystic tradition began to fade. In the eighteenth century its voice could hardly be heard. Today, if we are to explore spiritual stillness we must go to the disciplines of the East. Some who go accept fully an eastern life style. For the rest of us these journeys to the East give us deep experiences, but there comes a time when we must return and dig for the roots of our own traditions.

A CONTEMPORARY NEED

People meditate for many reasons. It is a process that accomplishes many different things. I meditate because it is a way of learning to listen to myself. One of the differences I find in what I hear through meditation and through the other avenues by which I listen to myself is that in meditation I experience the language of the world of me, and in the other avenues the messages are translated into the language of symbols and words that are more familiar to my conscious self. In meditation it is harder to listen, but what I hear is often stronger than with other methods.

I have selected from the various methods of meditation an approach that best helps me listen to my inner world. There is a tendency in me and in many of us who approach meditation or other means of self-awareness to go faster than we should; to go beyond a method before we have really experienced it. I have learned that there is a positive value to staying with one approach past the time when it seems as if its utility has been maximized. This has been an important lesson in my attempts to experience the world of me.

Although I find it a unique experience to meditate with a group, many of my meditations take place when I am alone.

Even if you cannot spend thirty to forty minutes a day, it is good to have even a five-minute period set aside each day for some meditation.

Select a place where you will not be interrupted. It does not have to be a place completely free of noise or distractions. Outside sounds are merely observed like your own thoughts. "No need at all of hills and streams for quiet meditation," advises the ancient sage. "When the mind has been extinguished, even fire is refreshing."

It is important to begin a meditation in a relaxed and balanced position. Sitting on a pillow enables you to have a more balanced, straight position and to be more comfortable for the period of the meditation. If sitting on the floor is difficult, use a chair. The precise position is not as important as the attitude it encourages. The old instructions to the Buddhist disciple still have merit. The disciple is told to "sit down." This way he assumes a posture that is calm, and that does not lead to sleep; neither does it encourage restlessness (5). It is recommended that he "sit cross-legged," because this is a firm and easy position for breathing. He is told to "keep the body straight," to hold the upper part of his body so that his spine is in a straight line.

Sit down and listen. Listen to the sounds in the room and outside the room. Do not play with the sounds. Just listen. Listening is not waiting. You are not going through a preliminary vestibule in order to get to the important stuff. When you are listening, you are meditating. Indeed, when you sit down you are meditating. Our daily lives are filled with noise and buzzings. When we listen, we are not continuing to buzz around. Meditation is not doing something more. It is the absence of something, just as a valley is the absence of a mountain. If we sit down to meditate and try to "get there" we are still climbing the mountain. When we sit down and are only sitting down, then we have stopped climbing the mountain. So we listen without listening for anything. We do not expect anything more to come. When we listen, we listen. We do one thing. For a moment we are like the old monk who described his spiritual path this way:

> When I eat, I eat.
> When I sleep, I sleep.

Now, become an observer of whatever is going on inside you. If you are bringing troubles or cares or joys or images into the meditation, do not try to push them aside, but observe them. Become like a withered tree. Resolve to do nothing. Watch your ideas. Notice how your thoughts and concepts follow one another. Say to yourself from time to time, "I am not my troubles," and then you will find your troubles or thoughts begin to move around you, and you become an observer. Watch your thoughts as you would observe a flock of birds flying overhead. Then you will sense a difference between you and what has been occupying your attention.

Gaze at the flame of a candle. Not to observe it or to attempt to control it or analyze it, but to try to merge with the candle flame; to surrender to its world.

After a few moments, focus upon your breathing. The purpose of counting breaths is to cut off mental activity and become passive—stabilized. There are many specific approaches to breathing exercises. I will describe one. The variations come naturally after you have practiced this method.

Even though in Zen the student meditates with open eyes, I suggest you begin by closing your eyes. Become conscious of the process of breathing. Feel the air as it comes in, goes through and out of your body. Become aware with each breath of how the air travels throughout your entire body. After becoming truly aware of this process, concentrate on exhaling; on pushing the air out. And as you push the air out, push all the air out. You will find that the air comes in naturally, by itself. It comes to you. Exhale slowly and completely, getting all the air out of your lungs. Follow each breath as it goes out. You will begin to feel a downward motion in the body as you exhale. Then, as you exhale, silently count each breath. Count from one to ten as you feel this downward motion. If you become distracted, start the count over. In other words, if you have counted up to five, and your mind becomes active, then begin again with one. When you have counted to ten, then also begin again, and count again from one to ten. As you continue this process, there are many opportunities to become involved with visions and ideas. This exercise is like an elevator. You can continue to go down, or you can elect to get off. In order to help you continue it is useful in groups for someone from time to time to say "continue to count," or to strike a small bell or block of wood to convey the same meaning.

Many more words could be used to describe what happens in a meditation of this sort, but they would have little meaning to anyone who had not tried this experience.

It is important that a meditation not be judged. Do not consider what happens as being either good or bad, and accept it. In this way you can listen. If you find yourself judged in a conversation, you do not speak as freely. The judgment can be either good or bad; you feel an automatic restriction. It is similar in listening to yourself. If the self is judged, there are restrictions in communication. If you are judging during a meditation, then observe your thoughts; observe the judging, just as you observe your other thoughts or troubles. "In the landscape of Spring" goes the old saying, "there is neither better nor worse—the flowering branches grow naturally, some long, some short."

In the group meditations at the Humanist Institute, individuals come quietly into a room lit only with a candle. We sit in a circle. We listen. We observe our own thoughts and dissociate ourselves from the toys with which our minds have been occupied. Then we focus upon the candle and attempt to merge with it. Someone then asks us to close our eyes, begin the process of becoming aware of our breathing and to start counting our breaths. For approximately thirty minutes, we are reminded about every five minutes to continue to count. We frequently end with a simple chant.

AFTER YOU BEGIN

It is necessary for you to start meditating before you can look for meaningful assistance or guidance in the use of this tool. Most books are not helpful. There are a few exceptions, such as Chogyam Trungpa's excellent little volume, *Meditation in Action* (6) and Shunryu Suzuki's gentle book, *Zen Mind, Beginner's Mind* (7).

After a few weeks of daily meditation you might find some of the following concepts helpful. They will make very little sense if you read them as you have been reading the preceding paragraphs. When you are ready, slowly look at each item as if you were examining shells on a beach.

Slow down. Do not approach meditation with excitement, but with awareness.

There is silence within noise. Anything that appears to interfere with your perfect meditation can be an opportunity for growth and training. A light is more easily found in the darkness.

There are days when there is a haze between you and the flower. The flower is there. If you stop striving, if you stop trying to see, you can smell the fragrance.

There is a Tibetan admonition not to copy the unskilled farmer who throws away his rubbish and buys manure. The wiser farmer collects his rubbish, works it, spreads it on his land, plants his crops.

Pain, joy, fear, indeed any event or emotion is to be examined, not by analysis but with a detached awareness.

"How do you get emancipated?" the monk asks the Zen master. The master replies, "Who has ever put you in bondage?"

"A day," says Meister Eckhart, "whether six or seven ago or more than six thousand years ago is just as near to the present as yesterday. Why? Because all time is contained in the present now-moment." He also teaches that "one idea is so like another essentially that it is impossible to distinguish between them."

You have everything you need. You are all you need. If you are centered you will not expect anything from anyone else. You will not depend upon others and because you do not need, you are free to want and to love.

If you become truly skilled in meditation, you will be able to approach each session with the simplicity and naiveté of a beginner.

There is a Zen tale: A new monk asked a master to teach him. The master says, "Have you eaten your rice porridge?"

"Yes," says the monk. "Then wash your bowl," says the master. At that moment the monk was enlightened.

The purpose of meditation is not to obtain a higher state or to gain anything, but simply to experience what is here and now, to become aware of a state and moment that I already possess.

You should not meditate in order to be enlightened. Meditate to be yourself. Sometimes Buddhist teachers say "Kill the Buddha!" Meister Eckhart said, "Sometimes for the love of God you must leave God." What you are looking for you already have.

LIVING IN MY PRESENCE

There is a Buddhist saying, "The instant you speak about a thing you miss the mark."

It is frustrating to try to describe or to read in words something that is basically a nonverbal experience; and yet, not to try to verbalize the experience leaves the practice of meditation with its unfortunate connotation of being a very special practice not available to many people.

To learn about meditation, you meditate. It is simple to begin, and you learn with each meditation about the next step. My purpose is to give enough of a background to let you feel free to commence the process of meditation, and it is hoped that those who find these words useful will train themselves by meditating and then speak to others who have had similar experiences, in order that the richness can be shared. An important part of the process is to learn detachment; what the Stoics and Christian Desert Fathers called *apatheia* ("passionlessness"). In this process we learn not to be controlled or possessed by our emotions. There will always be distractions in meditation. This is a natural, and perhaps necessary, part of living. If a dog barks as I meditate I become angry. But the anger does not come from the dog, it comes from me; from my desire to have things in a certain way, my desire to control. Now there is nothing wrong with having this desire, and it would be wrong to attempt to deny that the desire is there. Yet I can detach from the desire and refuse to become its slave.

To me, the simplest definition of meditation, and at the same time the few words that give the greatest challenge, are contained in an ancient definition of the word "zazen":

> Outwardly, to be in the world of good and evil, yet with
> no thought arising in the heart, this is Sitting (za);
> Inwardly, to see one's own nature and not move from it,
> this is Meditation (zen).

It is hard for me to be in the world of good and evil and not have thoughts rising in my heart. It is vital to me that I inwardly see my own nature, and most important, that I not move away.

VII

From the Occult

7

MYSTICISM IS A process of gaining knowledge, wisdom, or insight by direct experience. This usually means a long process of disciplined contemplation and awareness. The mystic sees mental reasoning and logic as only one avenue to understanding, and not necessarily the best.

My wisdom is not just in my head. There are many other wise parts of me; my memories, my inner world, my total gestalt and organic being, can all provide me with wisdom. All nonmental approaches to understanding are difficult for us today. Jung has observed:

> What Psychologists call psychic identity, or "mystical participation," has been stripped off our world of things. But it is exactly this halo of unconscious associations that gives a colorful and fantastic aspect to the primitive's world. We have lost it to such a degree that we do not recognize it when we meet it again. With us, such things are kept below the threshold; when they occasionally reappear, we even insist that something is wrong (1).

Regaining this knowledge has been the task of many mystics. Although the tradition is more prevalent in the East, we have had quite a number of mystics in the West. African cultures have produced mystics and in the case of the Bushmen perhaps mysticism is the dominant approach to life (2). If we look at the tradition in this fashion, we can add to the list: Hermann Hesse, Carl Jung, many contemporary psychologists and religious leaders, as well as most modern poets.

Mystics search themselves in order to gain knowledge and wisdom. This inward search is related to the concepts of self-exploration as used in this book.

The word "occult" comes from roots related to "conceal." Through the ages occult practices have come to mean shortcuts to mystical experiences, knowledge, or power. Some of the occult practices can be helpful as tools of self-exploration.

ABUSING THE OCCULT

There are a number of misuses of the occult in common vogue.

In this age of mass alienation the occult grows in popularity. People try to overcome loneliness by believing that the stars are interested in them. The universe becomes the family, and more nourishing ways of gaining a sense of belonging are avoided. The extreme is to be found in the cults and secret societies that have found the magic pill; THE answer. These people worship the tool rather than use it.

The people-helpers who use the occult as an attractive trick are also misusers of the occult. In this there is an arrogant lack of respect for the rich aesthetic dimensions of the occult process.

In approaching the occult a person often has such strong preconceptions that he can not hear what is being said.

ALCHEMY

Many parts of the occult are related to our contemporary search for full understanding of the human potential. Alchemy has received considerable attention. The alchemist was a chemist and a mystic. On the surface it would appear that the alchemist is looking for ways of making gold from other metals through the use of a "philosopher's stone." But

Jung found alchemical symbolism in the dreams of some of his patients, and it led him to a study in which he concluded that the alchemist was not really reexploring the nature of matter, but his own unconscious mind.

> The real nature of matter was unknown to the alchemist; he knew it only in hints. Inasmuch as he tried to explore it he projected the unconscious into the darkness of matter in order to illuminate it. In order to explain the mystery of matter he projected yet another mystery— namely his own psychic background—into what was to be explained: *Obscurum per obscurius, ignotum per ignotius!* [The obscure is to be explained by the more obscure, the unknown by the more unknown.] This procedure was not, of course, intentional; it was an involuntary occurrence (3).

Through alchemy a person moved himself from a material to a spiritual state, either for its own sake, or because he had to in order to obtain the gold. The medieval sage advises: "Out of other things thou wilt never make the one until thou hast first become one thyself."

The path was a long and hard one requiring total commitment. Great wealth was never produced. It is possible that none was ever intended to be manufactured. What did result was some knowledge about the physical and spiritual universe, and a considerable understanding by each alchemist of his own inner world.

TOOLS FROM THE OCCULT

Two ancient devices for divining the future that can be used practically for self-exploration are the western Tarot the eastern *I Ching*.

THE TAROT

The Tarot cards are the ancestors of our modern playing cards. Many members of occult sects believe that the cards date back to the Egyptians and hold spiritual knowledge. The story is that the cards were given to the Gypsies as a bible, but they were also a means to gain their livelihood by telling fortunes. In this fashion, the meaning of the Tarot was kept alive, even though the guardians did not know its full meaning (4).

Probably the cards were more medieval in origin. There are no known decks before that time. The deck is divided into two parts called Arcana. The major Arcana consists of twenty-two cards. The minor Arcana has four suits: cups (hearts), wands or staves (clubs), money or pentacles (diamonds), and swords (spades). Each suit has fourteen cards: king, queen, knight, page (jack), and numbered cards from ten to one (ace).

The Tarot is used for many purposes, usually entertainment and fortune-telling. It can also be used as a key to the philosophy of life embodied in a number of ancient writings. The cards can, for example, be related to the Tree of Life in the Cabala of medieval Jewish mysticism. In that framework, the major cards represent twenty-two paths or roads in man's spiritual journey.

The person studying the Tarot moves through several stages of understanding. Finally, he has the use of a rich tool of self-awareness, in addition to any other benefits he might have gained. To begin, a good book and a good teacher are needed, both of which are rare. The classical work on the Tarot was written by Papus in the nineteenth century. This contains a considerable amount of informa-

tion if you are willing to tolerate the intentional obstacles
the author puts in the way of the uninitiated. A brief but
clear overall statement is found in Richard Cavendish's *The
Black Arts* (5).

Few people are willing to engage in a major study -of
the Tarot. I have attempted to design a tool of self-exploration based on the Tarot. It is not the essence of the Tarot
nor is it a trick for psychological insight.

THE TAROT AS A TOOL

You need to purchase a Tarot deck. Get the ancient
Marseilles deck. The more common Waite deck and most
of the modern decks are cluttered with private and cult symbols.

Use only the cards of the major Arcana, the cards numbered 0 through 21. Shuffle the cards as much as you like.
Do not ask a specific question unless you have one that is
strongly preoccupying your attention. Assume that you will
learn something about the present state of your growth.
This insight will be in the form of a sharper focus on where
you have been, where you are, and where you will go (the
implication of where you are).

As you lay down the cards, do not reach for meaning
or manufacture explanations. Try only to hear your immediate inner response. If you hear nothing, go on to the
next card.

Put the deck face down in front of you. Draw a card,
turn it over, and put it down. This first card is the issue to
which the cards will speak. Put down nine other cards in
the following manner:

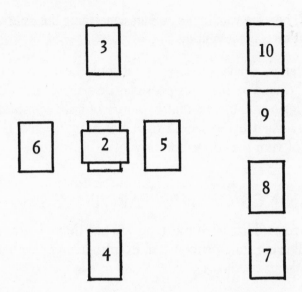

Let the cards represent the following positions or facets of the issue:

1. The issue.
2. What crosses you, or gets in your way.
3. What crowns you; the highest aims or goals that can be obtained.
4. What is at the base of you; something that is basic in you.
5. What is behind you; where you have been.
6. What is before you; a general statement of what is to come.

The next four cards are more specific:

7. This is where you are now in relation to the issue.
8. This is the environment in which you are working on the issue.

9. These are your hopes or fears concerning the issue.
10. This is the resolution.

After you have finished laying out the cards, let your mind become as blank as possible. Be passive. Look at the cards again one by one and be aware of your immediate reactions. Then try to see all the cards together and become aware of your overall reaction.

MEANINGS OF THE TAROT CARDS

Each card has what meaning you put there. I have found the following statements useful in introducing people to the Tarot.

XXI *The World.* Moving to a higher level, joy, release.

XX *Judgment.* The judgment day. Calling forth unexercised parts of me. Awakening my spiritual nature. Aspiration.

XIX *The Sun.* Taking a direct path in the sunlight. Knowing where I am going.

XVIII *The Moon.* Taking a dark path, an unknown way.

XVII *The Star.* Hope. No destruction is final. No fall is irreparable. Renewal, revival.

XVI *The Tower of Destruction.* False hope. Putting all my focus into one thing. Becoming a true believer. Lacking balance.

XV *The Devil.* I am bound by my desires, pride, or ambition.

XIV *Temperance.* Slow down. A flow or balance.

XIII *Death.* Spiritual decay. The possibility of a new life.

XII *The Hanged Man.* Destruction of the false self. Submission to higher things.

XI *Force.* Strength and vitality. Feeling one's own strength. Exhibiting it in an effortless way.

X *The Wheel of Fortune.* Making all manner of things go at once. Living with the implications of one's deeds.

IX *The Hermit.* The man who must be alone if he is to continue. He must do it himself. The teacher within has been found and must be heard. Still this man can be a light to others.

VIII *Justice.* Equilibrium. Stern commands to move from the abstract to the practical in an honest fashion and cleanse myself of warring tendencies.

VII *The Chariot.* The competing inner forces are now working together. I begin to move.

VI *The Lover.* Two roads meet. Do I use what I have learned to go on to the spiritual life, to continue to work on myself? Or do I stop and use my power to master or impress those who have not done the things I have?

V *The Pope.* The teacher of higher things. Spiritual authority.

IV *The Emperor.* Active. Order. Domination over material problems.

III *The Empress.* Linking the active and the passive. The natural path is an easy path. Balance and flow.

II *The High Priestess.* She has knowledge of all that is truly important. Dualities become one. She is the gate.

I *The Magician.* The expert juggler. Unity. Control over all elements. Directing force.

0 *The Fool.* Divine folly. The free spirit.

I CHING

The *I Ching* has a collection of sixty-four groups of lines. There are two basic lines; the yang (———) and the yin (— —) . The lines form a language probably preceding words. In ancient China combinations of these lines were formed into an elaborate system of fortune-telling with a specialized priesthood. In an effort to return the oracle to the people, the *I Ching* or *Book of Changes* was put together. Much later, Confucius added verbal commentaries, and many who followed him composed additional comments. The *I Ching* is truly Chinese. It emphasizes the ever-changing rhythm of life. Bad times today are part of a good tomorrow.

THE FAMILY

There is a family of eight members in the *I Ching*. All eight are also found in each of us. Each of these members is symbolized by three lines (a trigram) . The following are the lines, names, descriptions, and images of the family.

CH'IEN, the father.
Strong and creative.
Heaven.

K'UN, the mother.
Accepting and receptive.
Earth.

CHÊN, the first son.
Shaking and arousing.
Thunder.

K'AN, the second son.
Dangerous and abysmal.
Water.

KÊN, the third son.
Stillness and rest.
Mountain.

SUN, the first daughter.
Gentle and penetrating.
Wind and wood.

LI, the second daughter.
Clinging and beautiful.
Flame.

TUI, the third daughter.
Pleasure, joy, and happiness.
Lake.

THE HEXAGRAMS AND THE CHANGES

The eight trigrams are combined into sixty-four hexagrams. What happens when two members of the family meet creates the moment in the dramatic story of the *I Ching*.

In order to use the *I Ching*, you throw yarrow sticks or coins and by a predetermined formula of numbers form six lines. Some of the lines in the original hexagram change; yang become yin, and yin change to yang. In this way a second hexagram is formed, which completes the message of the *I Ching*. Although the explanation is complicated, the system is considerably less difficult than the Tarot.

AS A TOOL

You will need a book, and I would recommend two. The standard work is the Wilhelm/Baynes translation, which contains an introduction by Carl G. Jung (6). It places a heavy stress on the commentaries, and is a good book, even though it tends to be rather ponderous and sacred. At the other end of the scale is a recent work by Gia-Fu Feng (7). This is an earthy and mod version emphasizing the lines and the simple message.

The normal way of obtaining the lines is by casting coins. This way is used because it is faster, but be careful not to go too fast. The process is important. Watch the lines develop and be aware of your reactions.

Get three coins. Traditionally heads are yin and tails are yang. Yin count as 2 and yang as 3. Throw the coins and count the results:

6 means an old yin   ▬ ▬
7 means a young yang   ▬▬▬▬
8 means a young yin   ▬ ▬
9 means an old yang   ▬▬▬▬

The difference between 6 and 8 is that 6 changes into a yang to form the second hexagram. Nine is also a moving line and changes into a yin in the second hexagram.

Unlike the Tarot, the question here is important. Think of your question, refine it, and make it simple and basic. Write down your question. Work with it some more. Is this really the question? Can you answer it? Is there a question behind this one? Work until you have a basic question.

Imagine that you have come into the presence of many wise old men. They listen for your question. The old men will talk among themselves and to you. In order to learn what they are saying, do the following:

Cast the coins six times. Each time (starting at the bottom) draw the line. It is customary to mark the changing lines (6 or 9) ——X—— or ——O——. I prefer to mark on the side X—— ——or O——so as not to distort the lines.

After you have formed the hexagram, become passive. Look at the lines. See if the lines themselves cause a reaction. Next think of the lines as a combination of two trigrams. Think of them as symbols for two members of your inner family who are now combined.

Finally, go to the book and read the commentary. On the first hexagram there will be a general statement followed by a particular comment according to which lines change.

Then draw the second hexagram. Begin at the bottom. Draw slowly. Copy the young yin and yang lines. Change the old yin and yang lines (6 and 9). Now repeat the procedure you used for the first hexagram except that there are no specific comments for the lines in the commentary. Then sit passively and look at both hexagrams. See them together. Hear the message of the old men.

Regardless of how an occultist may have expressed it, he was in the process of getting in touch with what was within him. Perhaps this was not all, but this had to come first. The tools suggested above can help us do the same thing. The pictures, images, and thoughts presented by the Tarot and *I Ching* are many. What I choose to see and hear at any given moment is an indication of where I have been, am now, and will be if I stay on this course. Someone else could look at the same thing and hear something entirely different.

These ancient tools also have their own aesthetic reality. Through many years they have been refined to focus on vital human questions. If I let them speak I can not only see where I am, but also obtain some well-seasoned advice.

VIII

More Tools

IN THE FOREGOING chapters we have looked at a number of tools of self-exploration that are of general importance to many people. Among the following brief descriptions of other tools used by some people you may find one that has particular significance for you.

CHILDHOOD RECOLLECTIONS

Childhood memories have been used by many psychological schools as part of the therapy process. Adlerians saw childhood recollections as a way to become aware of your life style. They observed that a person's childhood recollections change as his life style alters. A variation of the therapeutic model can be used as a self-exploration tool.

What is your earliest childhood recollection? Try to get a quick flash. Think of two more. Record the three scenes as if they were something you saw on a movie screen—"I am sitting at a table in the kitchen looking at the snow outside. I am alone." Do not get into how you felt then. After you have recorded the three scenes, try to find a common theme. If you have trouble, involve a friend. The thread could be anything. Do not be surprised at anything. Be open to very simple messages.

Try to recall preschool situations. If you are having difficulty, think of your first day of school. Whether the memory is actual, a photograph, or even a fantasy makes no difference. You can hear the story of your childhood in many ways. I find the following an always enriching exercise.

Take pencil and paper; think of a childhood home, and

live in the home again. See all the things. Taking your time, draw the floor plan of the home. There is often a flood of memories, many of which relate to what is going on with you at the present time. Frequently, there is a memory connected with the house that contains some advice for the present. Remember you are not trying for accuracy, but to hear the story that is inside at this moment.

A LETTER TO YOU

One of our perennial difficulties is being simple. A way of hearing a message from the inner world in basic terms is to do something that cannot become sophisticated. Try doing this exercise now:

Take a piece of paper and a pencil. Decide that you are going to write a letter to yourself. Write on a simple topic, "What I want today," or "What I did last week." Put the pencil in your nondominant hand. For most, this would mean using the left hand. Do not plan anything. Address the letter to you, put "Dear _____," write the letter, and then sign it. Fold the letter. Sit quietly for a moment. Be still and passive. Open the letter. Read it. Hear it. These childlike letters are quite moving, even months later. The letter does not look like the normal me, but I know it is me. That scrawl, those ideas are in me. They are me.

MOVEMENT

When I am uptight, my body is uptight. If I am standing or sitting, my body will show the tension. Reading bodies is a natural phenomenon in encounter groups. A person sitting with arms and legs crossed is not believed when he says he feels open. I can learn to read my own body. Just as my drawings or fantasy can tell me who I am, so can my body.

Put a record on the phonograph, one without words and a sound that is not extremely familiar to you. As soon as the music starts, begin to move. Do not stop until the recording stops. While you are moving do not dance. Do not construct anything. Imagine a ball in your right hand. Feel it. Pass it to your left hand. Throw it back and forth. Let your body sway with the throw. Any time while the music is on that you feel lost or contrived, go back to throwing the ball.

When the music has stopped, just drop your arms and rest. Be aware of what is going on with your body. Are you tight, loose, coordinated, or jerky? What is your body saying? If you start the sentence "I am _____," simple words often come to finish the statement.

There are a number of physical methods that not only help me listen to myself but also help me change. They begin to work on personal development via the body. My body cannot get loose unless I get loose. When I stop holding back physically, I will give emotionally. Two major approaches to using movement as a self-exploration tool are Alexander Lowen's Bio-Energetic Analysis (1) and Ida Rolf's Structural Integration. Women using the Lamaze method of child delivery alter their emotional attitudes by physical exercise (2).

The beautiful Chinese form of meditation, Tai Chi, also helps me get more centered. The Tai Chi master, Gia-Fu Feng, sees it as a bridge between eastern meditation and western psychotherapy (3). It gives a sense of flowing, of energy, of peace.

Tai Chi requires a period of instruction. The following is not Tai Chi, but some ideas from Tai Chi. Stand erect with your feet a bit apart. Close your eyes. Feel the weight of your hands. Let your hands hang. Rest. Become aware of your breathing; feel the air coming in and going out.

As you breathe in, let your arms come straight up in front of you. As you exhale, let your arms fall. Make your motions slow and smooth. As your arms go up, bend your knees. As your arms fall, straighten up. Do this for a while.

As you breathe in, let your hands pull the air to you. As you breathe out, push the air away. Repeat this motion many times in a rhythmic fashion.

Let your arms spread wide apart as you exhale. Cross your hands on your chest as you inhale.

After a while again let your arms come up and your knees bend as you inhale. Drop your arms and straighten your knees as you exhale. Do this for a while.

Feel the weight of your hands. Let your hands pull you to a position of repose. Rest.

PLAY

If you watch a child playing, you can tell a great deal about him. There is a child in you. When you let him out to play, you can learn a lot from him.

The difficulty with many group experiences that emphasize play is that the drive is to be childish, not childlike. Often people seem to use much time and money to construct a brattish representation of a child. These frenzied activities keep the child locked in. A child is not frantic; he knows what he wants.

We are often embarrassed to have others see the child emerge, so choose a secluded place. Let your hands move, play with paint. Go to a field and let your feet move. Let the child out; he will tell you what to do.

OTHER BOOKS AND PLACES

Many books are appearing that contain exercises for helping people grow in one way or another. A number of these have sections on self-exploration. Many of the exercises have little to do with personal growth, but do give a temporary feeling of heightened vitality. These seem somehow more appropriate for the program chairmen of service clubs or for the training of used-car salesmen. Books and groups that attempt to exploit the growing interest in the development of the human potential frequently emphasize the method rather than the process. Indeed, the gimmick is often put forward as a substitute or shortcut for growth. This present period is our adolescence. Let us hope that it is a short one.

√   Growth is connected with risk and no one can grow without being uncomfortable. As we begin to live again in the world of experience there are growing pains. Frequently, we assume that someone else has a more complete answer than what we can find in ourselves. However, if you have an honest, uneasy feeling about a book or a group, the chances are it is justified.

As we mature we will look for a process of authenticity.

If care is used, there are many additional sources for finding tools of self-exploration. Two of these deserve a special mention: Roberto Assagioli's *Psychosynthesis* and Laura Huxley's *You Are Not The Target*.

PSYCHOSYNTHESIS

Those who are uneasy with the lack of analysis in this book will find the approaches of psychosynthesis more comfortable. Although this school is a radical reaction to traditional psychotherapy, it still remains within the therapeutic approach. There are many similarities between Dr. Assagioli's book and this volume, especially the underlying assumptions about the importance of dialogue between the inner world and the conscious self. The approaches differ primarily in the following ways:

1. Dr. Assagioli is a therapist. His book speaks primarily of a therapist's relationship with his patients.

2. Psychosynthesis has a definite, very specific, philosophical model of man.

3. Fantasies and other techniques are seen as quick flights to the inner world to gather information to help the conscious self obtain more understanding.

4. There is a heavy emphasis on scientific inquiry, precise language, and understanding what has happened. Dr. Assagioli strives for systematic explorations of the unconscious.

5. There is an emphasis on getting at things in a quick and efficient manner. The following exercise is an example of those described in Dr. Assagioli's chapter on "Spiritual

Psychosynthesis—Techniques." The exercise is preceded by many pages of thorough explanation and followed by a guide for interpreting the various experiences that might occur.

The Blossoming of the Rose

We describe the exercise as it is presented to a patient or to a group: Let us imagine a rose bud, closed. Let us visualize its stem and leaves with the bud above. It appears green, because the sepals are closed, but at the very top a rose-colored point can be seen. Let us visualize this vividly, holding the image in the center of our consciousness.

Now begins a slow movement: The sepals start to separate little by little, turning their points outward and revealing the rose-hued petals, which are still closed. The sepals continue to open until we can see the whole of the tender bud.

The petals follow suit and slowly separate, until a perfect, fully-opened rose is seen.

At this stage let us try to smell the perfume of this rose, inhaling its characteristic and unmistakable scent; so delicate, sweet and delicious. Let us smell it with delight. (It may be recalled that religious language has frequently employed perfume as a symbol, e.g., "the odor of sanctity"; and incense is also used in many religious ceremonies.)

Let us now expand our visualization to include the whole rose bush, and imagine the life source that arises from the roots to the flower and originates the process of opening.

Finally, let us identify ourselves with the rose itself, or more precisely, let us "introject" it into ourselves. Symbolically we *are* this flower, this rose. The same life that animates the universe and has created the miracle of the rose is producing in us a like, even greater miracle—the awakening and development of our spiritual being and that which radiates from it.

Through this exercise we can effectively foster the inner "flowering" (4).

LAURA HUXLEY AND HER RECIPES

In Laura Huxley's lively little book she presents thirty-one recipes for converting bad energy into good! I have the feeling that Laura Huxley lives in another dimension and wrote this book while vacationing temporarily in the land of intellectual concepts and logical reality. It is delightful to find a book that contains almost no academic jargon. She encourages people to have faith in their creative imagination and to believe in their own organic strength.

Although many of her recipes are not so much tools of self-exploration as ways of living the good life, there are a number of valuable suggestions. You never get the feeling that Laura Huxley has *the* answer, and at times it does not even appear that she has a better answer, but she always suggests *an* answer. Perhaps the most necessary ingredient in her recipes is that she catapults the reader into the now. The process of leaving the discussion and moving into the experience frequently helps a reader find his own recipe.

The most commonly repeated phrase in her book is "It works, if you work." Here are some tools suggested by Laura Huxley's recipes, which will work if you work.

Questions. Often self-exploration is blocked because we

are not in touch with a question coming from the very center of our being. The question should be put to our whole being and does not come simply through our intellectual process. The answer can come from the same organic source. The first step is to hear and admit the question.

The following excerpts from Laura Huxley's recipes are from "Questions and How to Ask Them."

> Imagine yourself alone in a mountainous country. Throw your question to the sky and listen to the echo coming back to you from the surrounding crags . . . Close your eyes. Visualize a brilliant white wall. Write your question on the white wall. Look at your question. Make it disappear from the wall . . . Ask your question rhythmically with a tune when performing some muscular action like walking, exercising, beating eggs, cleaning the house . . . Dance your question . . . Ask your question to different parts of your body; ask your toes, and your spine, and your neck. Ask your eyes, your legs, your sexual organs, etc.

Silence. In her recipes, "Songs Without Words," Laura Huxley comes close to some concepts used in meditation. However, her suggestions are sufficiently different to warrant including here.

> Go to a place where you will be alone and undisturbed. Make yourself comfortable, sitting or lying down.
>
> Feel whatever is in you at the moment. If you wish, feel whatever feeling has lately been troubling you.
>
> Do not give a name to this feeling. Attach no words to it.
>
> Let the feeling fill you completely. Let it spread through all your being. Yet, observe it as if you were a bystander.

Sitting or lying down, inwardly still, let feeling flow through you like a stream of silence, a song without words.

If memories should emerge—faces, places, past events—don't interfere. Neither push them away, nor plunge into them. Only watch, and let them flow by.

What is My Model. It helps me to get a sense of where I am if I can become aware of who it is I want to be and what changes I want to take place in me. The following suggestion is one of a number that appear in the recipe "Your Imagination is Yours."

Close your eyes. Imagine a mirror.

Project, in that mirror, the image of yourself with the figure you can and wish to have; project yourself with the posture you can and wish to have.

I Am Not My Troubles. "Prajna" is a Sanskrit word meaning "an ever present state of grace." This grace is not to be obtained by effort. Prajna is in us now and is to be accepted and realized. I lose touch with Prajna when I let my troubles control me, define me; when to all intents and purposes I am my troubles and nothing else. I say to myself occasionally, "I am not my troubles" as a way of breaking through my preoccupation. Similar suggestions are made in the recipe "Prajna Now." Laura Huxley suggests that I say to myself frequently and routinely that I am not my troubles. If I am sad, I remind myself that I am not only my sadness, so I say "I am not my sadness." But there is sadness, so I say, "There is sadness." I follow this quickly with the phrase "Prajna Now" and I mean now! Does this sound like a silly game and gimmick? Try it now (5)!

YOUR SPECIAL TOOLS

Develop some tools of your own. They may not work for everyone, but they will work for you. Test out your tools. When one brings you a piece of the puzzle, use another tool and see if the messages are related.

There is a temptation to change tools right when the message begins to make you nervous. This should be avoided or else you will get a great familiarity with all the hammers and never drive a nail.

IX

Groups

JOURNEYS TO THE inner world are basically an individual experience, but a properly organized group can be of assistance, particularly in providing an introduction to the tools and giving training in the necessary self-discipline.

There are two major problems that may develop in the group, both of which relate to the attitude of the leader. If the group is seen as a weekly turn-on opportunity, then the participants continue to cover the same ground until the first rung on the ladder collapses from overuse. Secondly, a participant can become dependent upon the group rather than getting training for life. If I can only listen to myself in the presence of a particular leader or group, I am not in touch with the strength within me. This dependency keeps me on the first step.

Provided the leader is not encouraging these situations, both of the foregoing problems and many others can be averted if one condition is made explicit. These groups are to be composed only of people who are committed to working daily on their own development. People who wish to work only during the weekly group should be asked to leave the group. The leader also should be seriously engaged in working on his own growth. It may be possible to lead many kinds of groups with insights based on past experiences. This is not such a group. If a leader is not presently working on a daily regime of self-exploration, he should not be leading the group.

CONVENTIONS

There are a number of types of weekly self-exploration groups. Some are limited to one particular tool, such as dreams or meditation. Each type of group develops its own procedures. The group with which I am most familiar is the Me Group of the Humanist Institute.

After about a year of experimentation, the Me Group was established in the fall of 1969 and has been a basic part of the program since that time. Each group meets once a week for ten weeks in two-and-a-half hour sessions.

Following are some of the conventions and assumptions developed in the Institute's experience with the Me Group.

1. The leader has two functions. He is a trainer in the use of the tools, which is majorly accomplished in the beginning sessions. He is also a facilitator to help the group flow and to share his knowledge and experiences. He is not a guru or a therapist. He leads by pushing himself, by taking risks. Leadership is not a shield against growth opportunities.

2. They are groups of workers. It is important for each participant to work daily in his journal.

3. The group focuses exclusively on training and experiences. There are no casual discussions, no abstractions, no head trips of any kind.

4. Perfect attendance is encouraged. Even missing one session, a person sometimes has a hard time catching up with what has taken place. If a person misses two times in succession (for whatever reason), he is not allowed to continue. The basic trust so necessary to a group is established if each participant knows that everyone is working. Casualness is a great detriment to the development of the necessary environment.

5. Groups should be small, between five and ten persons. Six or seven is the best size. Participants who have had previous Me Group experience should be put together. In experienced groups people can be paired. Each day the

partners can share their dreams of the night before, either in person or in a telephone conversation.

6. No one takes responsibility for anyone else. You move. No one will coax you. Each participant must take the first step himself.

7. No one "helps" anyone else. As I hear your experiences I let them come into me and affect me. I do not give you insight, but I share with you my emotional response to your experiences. In other words, I give you me, not thoughts about you. This is a difficult concept. Doing it calls for more personal risk than the approach of calculated insight. Questions of any kind are discouraged. In sharing myself it is more relevant to talk about myself. If I have no reaction I have nothing to share. If I feel that I am talking to a particular person, I am probably not sharing my emotional response.

8. When I share a dream or other experience, I no longer own it. What is before the group belongs to everyone. It is tempting for a participant to tell the group when he feels as if they are being accurate about a dream. Don't! It is burdensome to engage in the game of—is this close to the mark? If I feel something strongly, I get into the dialogue. Everyone speaks for himself. A fantasy on a dream can be more intense than the original dream.

9. The journey to the inner world is handled as a natural part of human existence. It is routine, not sacred.

THE PROCESS

Although each Me Group develops in its own way, the following is how a ten-week group of new people generally proceeds.

The first sessions are mainly devoted to training in the

use of fantasy and the journal. The journal is begun with some common experience. Everyone agrees to do two fantasies each day and record any dreams.

In the second session the experiences in the journals are shared. Training in other tools of self-exploration is explored, such as art. And in the third session the group begins to work with dreams.

By the fourth session most of the participants have the central idea of self-exploration. The path is frequently so new and so rewarding that everyone indulges himself and is not interested in anyone else's experience. To handle this phenomenon people are encouraged to intensify their quest and to work harder. Gradually the participants realize that their discoveries are not fragile, and that they can become involved with the experiences of others without losing their sense of themselves.

When the group hits its stride and the leader becomes simply an experienced participant, the tendency to talk primarily to the leader stops and the intensity of the group picks up. There is seldom enough time to handle all the experiences participants want to share.

At this point a typical session would include working with materials in the journals. Participants bring in experiences and use the group to help get a clear focus on what the tools have produced. These are often not lengthy episodes. First reactions are the most valuable. For example, a group may react with laughter to an experience a participant has made into a melodrama. The lighter view will help the person hear the message. After many have shared some experience, a particular common experience will often suggest itself, such as a fantasy structure that everyone will react to and share in the group. These are good in themselves and also help bring into focus the shared experiences of the earlier part of the session. The session often ends with a personal time, such as group meditation.

After you have shared an experience, it is helpful to record the reactions of others. If you listen you will feel little reaction to some comments and a strong response to others. Write down these latter reactions next to the place you have recorded your experience in your journal.

ESTABLISHING A GROUP

If you are near an established group, you can try it. The foregoing comments can also serve as guidelines for setting up your own informal group.

Choose a friend with whom you would like to work in this way. The two of you choose a third, and the three choose a fourth. Stop at four or at the most five. It is important that the guidelines in the book be generally followed and that there be a common commitment that (1) you will meet at a definite time on a regular basis, (2) that all will work daily, (3) that there will be no small talk at sessions. Watch each other to make sure you are sharing your reactions, not just analyzing yourself or someone else.

A group is not to help you understand but to hear. It is also a way of truly committing yourself to using the tools of self-exploration. During the early days of the Me Group a participant wrote a letter to himself about this commitment. It is a letter we should all receive:

Are you willing to persist at a task until you learn and master the skills involved? This is not a turn-on, not a bunch of techniques that I can read about and then try out one time to see if I get the same result. The task is living in my own world, living in all my richness and depth. The tools and skills are a major part of a life style that is mine; they are valuable not for a month or a year, but for my whole life.

Things are happening and changing for me. For the past several months I have been standing back and observing and asking why. It has been a dead end. I ask, "Why?" and then "What ought to be?" and then "What should I?" and then I am back at "Why?" again. The inspiration and the living are not in asking why but in experiencing what is happening and what I am doing.

X

A Session

10

THIS IS A transcript of an evening meeting of a Me Group at the Humanist Institute. Ruth is an artist. Marshall is a young psychiatrist. Donald was in business and is now a student. Barbara is a full-time mother and a part-time typist. I am leading the group. There is a wide range of ages. The participants have all been in encounter groups. Some have worked with a particular tool of self-exploration, but none has been in a Me Group before. This is the fifth session of the group. This session is presented not because anything out of the ordinary happened, but because it is a typical session (1).

RUTH

I have a Statue fantasy.

I am standing in a clearing in a forest. I am vague. I am undefined. Around me there are small plants and animals, clearly and sharply defined. I try to bring myself into focus, but I remain a shadowy figure.

BARBARA

Could you repeat it, please.

(Ruth repeats the fantasy.)

DONALD

I'm dissatisfied. Life abounds around me. I am transparent and shadowy. I want definition.

MARSHALL

I feel safe. I am mysterious. I keep myself hidden. I want that, I want it that way. I want to be hidden from others. I don't want to be hurt. I don't want to be vulnerable.

TOLBERT
This is a Wall fantasy.

*I am standing looking at a shingled wall. I look at the
shingles and I daydream. I don't look for the door. I find the
door by accident—it's a little, wooden, arched door. I enter. I
don't look ahead. I look sideways, I look down, I look up.
Finally I am aware of being in a room. It is white and stark.
On the table is a bright, goosenecked lamp. I go to it—it's
shining on an article—it's a mirror. I see me, I am focused, I
pick up the mirror and I return.*

RUTH
I am disappointed. I went a long way to find what I already
had.

MARSHALL
I'm not looking for anything. Everything is the same. I find
the door. I go in. I won't look at anything. I'm not interested
in looking at anything. I see an article. I am curious. I pick
it up, I look at me. I am interested. I am very interested.
Looks important. I am interested in looking at me.

DONALD
I'm the goosenecked lamp. "I'm turned on myself—I'm
turned around. Lighting myself."

TOLBERT
I'm the mirror. "I'm cold, I am flat, I am beautiful in my
coldness, sharp—I reflect light."

BARBARA
I feel cold and naked and vulnerable.

(pause)

I have a Box fantasy.

A box from the store was left for me on the living-room table. I'm surprised. I come in, untie the ribbon around it, open it up. Inside there is a warm, soft cape that fits around my shoulders and ties around my throat. I put it on because I am chilled. It feels warm and soft.

TOLBERT

I'm nervous. I'm jittery. I'm angry. I didn't ask for anything. I open it; it's stroking me, it's soothing to me, it's pampering me, it's giving me rewards I'm entitled to, I deserve this, I deserve every minute, I love it.

DONALD

I have an Old Man fantasy.

An old man is sitting in a small reed boat in a river. I go to the boat and sit down beside him. He reaches his hand into a small leather sack and brings out a small handful of jewels. He hands me several. I smile and don't look at them. I ask him, "How will my health hold up?" He looks at me and raises both arms up in the air and says nothing.

TOLBERT

I hurt. I want to go up to these people. I want to see what they have to say, they look wise. This seems like a good moment. I have a feeling of peacefulness and specialness. But I've got one thing on my mind, that's the only thing that counts for me right now.

MARSHALL

I can give him jewels; I can't answer his questions.

TOLBERT

I'm up in the air. I don't know what I've got in my pocket, I don't want to look at what I've got.

RUTH

I have all these jewels in my hands and I'm asking for something—I'm not looking at the diamonds I already have, I'm searching for something else.

MARSHALL

I don't see what I have now. I don't value what I have now.

TOLBERT

I have to know about my health, that comes first. I've got to know about my health. I shouldn't even have come here.

BARBARA

I feel distracted. It's the basic things I want, and other things come in the way. They're distracting me.

TOLBERT

I resent this. I'm looking for a guy who's going to tell me if I'm going to be healthy, and I have to go out on a river and I've got to find three men in a tub to get any kind of answer from. They hand me some jewels and I want to know if I'm going to live or not.

MARSHALL

I have a dream.

Outside the stores of my childhood street I am running down a corridor. An old childhood friend is following or accompanying me. There are many lip colors to try on. I wish to put on a lip mask of soft wax. It is an old oriental art. I am

concerned about using someone's and that is a way of catching
a disease.

I am sitting in a restaurant with Laurel, then a Chinese
girl. We are eating. The food is very exotic but good. I have
difficulty talking to the Chinese girl. She is attractive, and we
do make ourselves somewhat understood. There is something
about her breasts, about needing help, about succoring. Other
people are now present. The dream ends.

RUTH

I like hiding behind my mask. Well, what if I get the wrong
mask? Something terrible might happen. And here I am in
this restaurant, and I don't even know what I'm doing here.
First with one girl and then another, I don't know who I'm
with or what I want. I feel confused, exposed.

TOLBERT

I don't know what I'm doing but I'm going to go along with
it, I'm going to act like I know what I'm doing. I feel like
this is a great honor to have the lip mask, so I will go with
that. I feel childlike, and I feel like I'm exploring a special
attic. I like what we're doing, I'll get the lip mask. It feels
funny, it feels strange, it could have some problems, I could
get somebody else's weaknesses. I'd really rather be speaking
with my own lips. I don't want someone else's, but I don't
know what to do. It's something of an honor somehow. I
don't understand what I'm eating. I would feel more comfortable if I knew what this was that I was eating, but it's all
right. I'm getting nourishment, but I don't know what it is.
I'm having trouble talking. I'm on unfamiliar ground. I'm
uncomfortable, but I'll go with it. This is not the street on
which I was born, this is not my street, this is different, but
it's all right—I think.

DONALD
I'm uncomfortable. This is not me. I'm paying lip service to something that I don't believe in. It's confusing to me.

BARBARA
It's a whole new world I'm growing up in, new customs, masks. I don't know what it all means.

MARSHALL
I want to make contact with this girl. I want to be understood. I want to understand her. I am attracted to her breasts. I am needing help. I think of needing help. I feel that I need to be fed. I am cautious about approaching this. I am cautious about going ahead with it. Other people are present, I can't go on with it. I have to go back to my masks, my lips. I want to be straight with what I want. I need help, I want help, I want nourishment, and I'm not making myself understood. It's difficult. I'm not coming across, we're not communicating. I'm put off. I'm easily put off from what I want, what I need. The other people are putting me off. I'm allowing them to put me off. I resent them for putting me off.

TOLBERT
I want help, I want nourishment, I want understanding. I want simple things and I want love. I want to belong. I want to be. I want to have my nest. I want to have my own lips. I want to have my own food. I want to have my own street.

DONALD
I have a dream.

There is a square house at the beach. It is tall and high over the surf. The weather is stormy and gray and cold. There is a

narrow, metal, open staircase and a ladder to the living area
on top of the house. I climb up—it's very scary. I enter. There
is a group of people milling around, sort of a party. I look out
the windows at the front. They are big and all across the house.
It is again very scary looking down. I climb back out across
manifold pipes and metal railings, and look down. Again I am
frightened. I climb slowly to the bottom and out to the beach
in front of the house. There are a few people walking around.
I go back inside on the ground floor and close the door. The
surf begins to pound against the front of the house. It moves
the door. I am concerned that the foundation will slip. I am
now upstairs again on the floor, and it is sloping. I am lying
down and feeling anxious that the building might tip forward
and over. I am now downstairs again and looking at the enormous concrete foundation and know that the building will not
tip over. The dream ends.

TOLBERT

I feel right. A beautiful, beautiful beach, not a straight line
in the whole place. Sandy, beautiful. There is a square house
right in the middle of it. It's out of place. I'm worried about
that house. I've got to keep that out-of-place house safe. I've
got to shore up that house. I have to keep it going. I'm
afraid to look. I'm afraid I'm going to lose. I'm going to slip.
I'm going to be out of control. I don't know what's on the
beach; I don't know what's around me. I'm afraid. My focus
is on the house. I am fearful; I am very fearful. I'm going to
slip away.

MARSHALL

I'm upstairs, I'm downstairs, I'm worried about it. It's
enough to drive me crazy. I'm anxious. Who needs it? I
don't want it here; I want to get rid of it. I can't get rid of

it, I'm trapped. I'm keeping the house up; the house isn't doing anything for me.

RUTH

I wish it would slip away, but it won't. I'm stuck with it. Look at that foundation, solid as a rock.

MARSHALL

I have an albatross around my neck. I want it. I don't want it. I don't really want it.

BARBARA

I'm shook up. I thought I was in a safe place, but now I'm being battered. Battered and battered, just battered all around. I thought I was safe, but it's not safe. Even if the foundation looks solid, it's still getting battered.

RUTH

I have a dream.

My daughter and I are in a large old house, brown with yellow trim. I am inside the house, but I can see it from the outside. It seems to be her house, and she is in a bedroom with a man. I don't know who he is. I am wandering helplessly through the house. I am supposed to go to work, but I don't know where or when. I go upstairs to the bathroom to finish dressing. There is a yellow tile floor with a drain. The whole room is yellow. The dream ends.

BARBARA

I feel bogged down from the pressures from responsibilities. I should be responsible for this person, for doing this, for doing that. I feel pressed by it.

TOLBERT

I'm confused. I don't know what's going on. I don't know what's happening. I *ought* to know what's happening, I *ought* to be on top of this, I *ought* to know who that guy is. I'm really not that interested. I *ought* to go to work; I don't know where. I *ought* to know where; I don't know what I'm doing. I really *ought* to know what is going on. I go in the bathroom. I am dressing. It's just me; I don't have to know anything. I know how to dress me. I know how to put clothes on me. I know how to get clothes for me. It is yellow. It is warm. I feel sunlight—sunshine. I am very nice. I am calm. This is just me. It's good.

MARSHALL

I'm split; I'm confused; I am inside and I am outside. I hear shoulds, shoulds, and shoulds and shoulds, and I don't care, I don't care, I don't give a damn. I want to do what I want. I should, I should do this, I should do that, and I want to do what I want, and I'm split, and I'm confused, and I'm trapped.

TOLBERT

I act like I know. I act like I should know. I act like I ought to know. I act like I am working. I have to know; I have to act like I know. It's required. It's heavy, it's burdensome. I can never let on I don't know; I've got to know. I've got to know. But, it's nice here, it's nice in the bathroom, it's nice just by myself. I don't have to know anything. (Pause) I want to be dumb. I want to be dumb. I don't want to know. I don't want to know who the guy is. I don't want to know where I have to work. I don't know what time I have to get there. . . . I know where the bathroom is.

TOLBERT

This is a wall fantasy.

I see a wall. My mind drifts away from the wall. I don't look at the wall. The wall is low and dull, stocky. It's a gray wall with an iron grate. I go on the other side of the wall and it's many walls, little walls. I recognize it as a maze and I back away.

MARSHALL

Repeat please.

(Tolbert repeats the fantasy.)

MARSHALL

I'm not interested. The wall is dull. Some things are dull. Some things I don't need to explore to find out. It's grating on me, so I go in, and it's a maze and I don't want to get sucked in. I don't want to play—it's dull, it's uninteresting. I go back. I don't care. I let things grate on me. I let things get the best of me. I get sucked in.

TOLBERT

If I just keep acting like it's not there, it will be all right. I can't move away from it; I don't have that power. I can't move. I'm being pulled in. There I go. Maybe if I don't look at it, maybe if I don't look at it, it will go away. I've got to go away. I have to turn away. I have to move away from the wall. I have to get away from the side of the wall.

MARSHALL

I have a dream.

I see Sid Boyle at an encounter group led by Tolbert. Tolbert gives us some pictures to put in frames. I want to

interact, encounter with Boyle. I am annoyed with Tolbert
for interrupting with the frames. I am annoyed with myself
for letting him. Boyle is obnoxious and probably drunk. I, too,
am scared and awkward. Tolbert is patient. It won't be too
hard to say goodbye to Boyle. People move about dancing—
close physical contact. Some girls are jealous of my attention.
There is a possibility of a fight. The scene changes. There is a
bar. My brother Dick is there. He is not well in focus. I am
overbearing with him as usual, impatient. There is an alterca-
tion. I am involved. I attempt to throw a customer over a
railing. Dick intercedes and prevents me by exclaiming, "He
is a truck driver who is concerned about an unruly employee."
A man, or I, stop a holdup later by pretending to have need of
the men's guns, thereby giving them an alibi to stop the
holdup. One of the girl encounter members was stabbed. The
Bay Area is rough to live in. A drunken, crazed man has stabbed
her. He mumbles, yells incoherently. I stagger to the party—
encounter group. I have two beers. I am drinking. The steps
are dangerous. I shove past people as I am running down the
steps. I get there. I don't want to be recognized by Martha.
I ask some operating-room girls from the hospital how the
party is. I don't want them to know I've been before. I'm
embarrassed. Gloria is there. She is very pretty. I am attracted
to her. I want to ask her to dance. I am annoyed about being
slightly drunk. The dream ends.

RUTH

Would you repeat, please?

(Marshall repeats the dream.)

RUTH

I feel bad. I feel guilty. I should have gone home too; I

shouldn't have come here in this condition, when I've had too much to drink. I'm no better than he is.

MARSHALL

I'm obnoxious. I'm a drunk. I'm overbearing. I'm impatient. I'm a holdup man. I'm a killer. I give alibis. I'm drunk. I'm mumbling. I'm yelling. I'm staggering. I'm dangerous. I shove.

TOLBERT

I'm going to kill this; I'm going to destroy this. I want to be drunk like Boyle—I don't want to be drunk like Boyle. I want Boyle to be sober like me. I want to be drunk like Boyle. I want Boyle to be sober like me. I don't know what's going on. They're going to find out I'm this way; I'm bad, I am a destroyer, I always destroy. They're going to find out. I'm embarrassed to tell them. I can't tell them, but they will find out. I'm feeling dull. I'm feeling heavy. I'm feeling hopeless. What's taking them so long to find out? I've been there before. Don't they know that?

MARSHALL

Find me out. Find me out. I'm drunk and I'm crazy; stop me. Stop me before I do this. Stop me. It's me, it's me; it's no one else. It's not this other man; it's me. I'm guilty. (Pause) Why don't I admit it's me? I'm the killer. I am a killer. Why do I hide it? Why don't I come out with it? I am a killer, a shover, a fighter. I'm drunken, I'm wild. I'm not guilty, I'm that way. I'm not guilty. I'm guilty. I'm guilty of it.

(Pause)

I am speaking for Boyle. I am drunk, and so what? I'm here where I want to be. I'm doing what I want to do. I don't need your moralizing. To Hell with you! To Hell with your moralizing. I'm drunk and I'm enjoying it.

RUTH

I feel sneaky. At least Boyle's honest about what he's doing.

RUTH

I wrote this to music.

Zow, wow now, stop eating me. Ooo, why play more. No I won't; I can't. This is the end. I don't care. Try to stop me; I go somewhere. I don't know. I can't tell. Now I go. Now I stay. I will tell, I will do what I will, I want, how, who, where. Blow the candle, light the light, the day is over. Will this never end? Walk the mile, climb the tree, go, stay, goodbye. I want to leave. I want to stand alone, no one near, far from all care, walking alone in the rain. Wet, soaking wet. Must get dry, can't get out of the rain. There is no shelter from the rain. Sunshine. Storm has ended. Warm and dry. Now I don't have to go.

BARBARA

Something's ending, something's beginning, something's ending, something's beginning.

TOLBERT

I like it out here. I like it in the rain, I like it in the wild, I like it in the rain. I'm all inside, I want outside. I want outside. I want in; I want out. I want in; I want out. I like it here where it's sheltered. I want to get away from the rain. I want to get away from the rain. I don't want to protect

myself. I want inside. I want outside. I want the wild. I want
the tame. I want the wild. I want the tame. I want the wet.
I want the warm. I want the wet. I want the warm, wet and
warm, warm-wet, warm-wet.

RUTH
I want to be wild and free. I want to be warm and safe.

TOLBERT
Warm and free, wild and safe, warm and free, wild and safe.
I want to be mixed up. Warm, free, wild, safe, safe, warm,
free, wild, safe, warm. What do I want? Where is it?

(Pause)

This is a dream.

*I am with Marti and Donny and Michael in a house. It's
raining outside. Outside is exaggerated perspective, like a
Breughel painting. There are fields outside; not quite planted.
Beautiful deer are walking in the fields. The dream ends.*

MARSHALL
I feel good. I feel good about my home. I feel good about
the setting, I feel good about the people inside. I feel comfortable. Outside, a time for planting, a time for work.

RUTH
I'm aware of the ground. The ground has been plowed. All
is ready for the planting. It would be nice to stay here in the
house and not have to go out and do the planting, but it
must be done. When you are going to have a crop later on,
you must do the planting now.

MARSHALL

I have to work for my nourishment, and it's a beautiful place to work for it. It's the right place, and that's the place I want to work. Everything is there.

TOLBERT

I am the deer. It's beautiful and it's wild. The rain is just stopping. There is no one out here but me. It's marvelous— every step I take is an adventure. Everything is fresh. Everything is new. Everything is beautiful. I am graceful; I am moving. I can see the house; I can see the people; I can see the fields. It feels good. It feels good, just being here.

DONALD

It's the spring. It's a new beginning. It's time to plant.

(Pause)

TOLBERT

Let's do a fantasy together; an island fantasy. You are on an island, get to the mainland.

(Long pause as people have and record the fantasy)

OK, let's share.

RUTH

I am on an island very like monkey island at the zoo. It is filled with labyrinths and caves. I run and hide and switch from one cave to another. I am having so much fun I don't want to return to the mainland.

TOLBERT

I am in a cave on an island. I am looking out at the ocean. It's a beautiful island. I am the only one on the island. I am walking out along the coral reef. I can vaguely see the mainland. There is deep water between me and the mainland. I don't want to move—I like the island. Do I really like the island? No. I want to get to the mainland. I am afraid. I am afraid to get off the island. I'll take a step. How do I really know it's deep? I won't guess. I'll take a step. Here I go.

MARSHALL

I am on a Pacific island with palms and a white beach and lush green undergrowth. The mainland is smogbound in the distance. I climb a tree, get, and then eat, a coconut. It's delicious. The water is warm and clear. I swim and look at the ocean floor. I want to explore the island. I am aware of being lonely.

DONALD

I am on a bulb-shaped island. The sky is dark and dreary. The only boat is wrecked and lying in shallow water. In the middle of the island is a tube that connects me to the mainland. I climb down into the tube and get in a small, yellow railway car. The tube is dark and clammy. Rickety, rickety, rickety, I roll down the tube in darkness under the water. Slowly the car slows and stops. Grope about and go up through a manhole into the sunshine on the mainland.

BARBARA

I am on a gem of an island with a beautiful blue sea, alone. There are beautiful green trees and hills and a sandy shore. Suddenly I see a beautiful ship coming. It's an ancient type ship with colored sails and men rowing. They land the boat

and greet me with great honor, carry me onto the boat, put me
in an honored seat, and row me back to the mainland.

TOLBERT

My strongest sense on listening to me was feeling so virtu-
ous, so noble. I have come in contact with my fear—I really
do want to get off the island. Then I go into this thing. I'm
sort of standing there with the most difficult possible way of
getting from one point to another; confronting the water,
pushing it back, step by step.

MARSHALL

Each step is going to be over my head. (Laughter) Will this
one do it? (More laughter) This is Russian Roulette, I
can't win!

RUTH

Oh, yeah, if I can hold my breath long enough, I can.

TOLBERT

Going out with real heroic virtue. They will mention this on
my tombstone . . .

DONALD

"That crazy guy!" (Laughter)

MARSHALL

My island was perfect. The only thing that was bugging me
was being alone, and I got in touch with my loneliness as a
barrier to self-exploration. I want to run from my loneliness.
My sense of loneliness makes me long for contact.

Ruth

I immediately felt very playful on your island, Marshall. I had the feeling that I could leave at any time I wanted to, but I didn't want to. The mainland was just a couple of steps away. It was really fun being there.

Barbara

I felt a sense of adventure in my fantasy from the minute I heard "island."

Tolbert

I had an all right kind of reaction to your fantasy, Barbara. I'm going to be taken care of. "Here they come." I felt a certain grandeur. There I go walking up the ceremonial stairs!!

Marshall

I am not going to concern myself with this problem. I am expecting my brigantine of guys to come along any moment.

Tolbert

I deserve it. I am being stroked, comforted, and taken care of, and it's about time!

Donald

My island fantasies are always nice and sunny and bright and typical islands. This one came up dark with heavy vegetation, and I saw that old, rickety boat half in the water, and I thought, "God, I want to get off this island." And then I remembered the tube that was there. In the middle of the beach I climbed down this concrete thing and got into the little car, like a little coal car that had some small tracks. I sit in it and I push it off, and I can see myself going down this slight grade under the water. It goes clickety, clickety, clickety click, and I'm kind of hunched over, going down this clammy tube. Then I got the feeling of a wind kind of going past my face, and it was dark and ominous.

MARSHALL

When you said you came up through the manhole cover I had the feeling I made it the hard way to get where I wanted to go. I have this filthy face and staring eyes, "I made it, I made it, I made it!"

TOLBERT

I had this picture of this idyllic setting with natives dancing, and in the middle up I come, bam! through the dirt, me and my coal car.

MARSHALL

I'm crazy, like in Stalag 17. People go crazy digging. It's their obsession, it's their compulsion, and they get a little bit mad inside there worrying about collapse. They look a little insane. I look a little insane.

(Pause)

I'd like to share another dream. It's in two parts.

I am in my old home with my brother Dick. There is confusion, darkness, activity. A question of illicit activities.

My brother and I are concerned about the ripped cape of my mother. She is very upset. We feel responsible. It is two black pieces of cloth with a red lining. We should get it resewn.

A woman is being made love to by a man in a car. It is an open affair. Some people see, some don't. Working in the outpatient department, it appears that patient services are now all prepaid, and Bill asks me if I approve of this. I tell him no, I like fee for services. A woman returns, mother, with an illicit affair. She was upset and her cape was ripped. Two black pieces of cloth, with an inner red lining, are not well sewn together. I think about the basting, temporary sewing for the cape. I am reluctant to repair the cape. I ask Carl if he will do it, or make an appointment for her to return it. The situation has calmed down. It is possible to think more clearly. Going through laboratory slips and bills, the urology service makes a lot of money. A nurse tells me what I ought to do before a patient and his wife. I am angry. I want to call a higher authority, but I am afraid he won't know me. The argument continues with the nurse. I know I should not get so involved, yet I want to let her have it. Another nurse offers calmer advice. Dr. Shirley McNeff is acting strangely. We, Donny and John and myself, really enjoy her. We cuddle up to her. She is very open and loving. She talks about another lover. I fantasize that I was her lover. I would like that. Now she appears ill. Her behavior is not in touch. We treat her as if she is very ill. Something bad has happened. I refuse to do a yellow sheet. I am annoyed by the resident. I yell. I try to control myself. He persists. I lunge at him. Even then I am aware of a scene. You shouldn't; it's a hospital. I back away. I apologize. Dr. Samuels is like a big daddy. We all gather around him. He plays with us. I tell Samuels about McNeff's behavior, and then it gets bizarre. She is like a goofy kid. The dream ends.

TOLBERT

I'm cautious. If you just don't pay any attention, if you don't care, if you don't invest yourself, it's all right. If you don't pay for what you get, if you don't put yourself into it. The pissing department gets a lot. It doesn't matter. That's the way the world is run; no investment, no caring, nobody putting out, getting something for nothing.

MARSHALL

I'm not responsible for my mother's crazy behavior. I'm not responsible for McNeff's crazy behavior. They're acting like kids. They're goofy, and I don't want to get sucked into something.

TOLBERT

I didn't rip the cape. I'm responsible, because it's my mother. I didn't rip it. I can't get the pieces together. It's not my kind of thing.

MARSHALL

The resident wants me to concern myself—write a history and physical, concern myself with the patient. I don't care! Stop hassling me! And I lunge at him. I'd like to strangle him. But I can back off. It shouldn't be done. God damn it, it shouldn't be done, so many shouldn'ts. It's a hospital so I should see the patient. It's my mother, so I should take care of her. To Hell with them; I'm not interested. I don't want any part of it. I don't want to be responsible for them.

RUTH

I feel ripped off, just like the damn cape.

DONALD

I feel confused. I want to repair the cape, I don't know how to repair the cape, better get somebody else to repair the cape. I want to strangle the guy, I want to strangle him. I want to go with it, I want to be able to go with it, I can't go with it. Confused. I want to stay with Samuels, I want to be protected. I want to be crazy like the woman. I want to be childish and crazy.

TOLBERT

I want to tell someone about the craziness. I want to let someone know. I want to talk. I want to let it out. I can't, I'm responsible. When I imagined I loved her is when the craziness started.

RUTH

I feel like giving up. It doesn't seem to do any good to tell them, they can't see what's there in front of their eyes. There's that couple in the car and they can't see it. They can't see anything! They only see what they want to see.

DONALD

My mother's going to be angry. She's going to put the blame on me.

BARBARA

I feel torn. I don't know how I'm going to mend me.

TOLBERT

How can I get together? How can I get the two sides together? How can I keep the rip from bleeding?

MARSHALL

I don't want to take care of the patients. I don't want to take care of my mother. I want to be taken care of.

TOLBERT

They aren't paying me anything. They aren't giving me anything. My mother's not giving me anything, the patients aren't giving me anything, I'm not getting anything. Dr. Samuels gives me something. I want to stay with him. I want to tell him all my troubles. I want to let him handle it.

DONALD

I want to work on a picture. (The drawing is of an egg in a nest.)

This is me. I am static. I am a large blue speckled egg and I am in my little straw nest. I'm hidden in the grass and I'm not coming out. It's cold and windy outside and I'm cozy in here. I don't want to move.

I want to try a dialogue.

- *(Left hand) I am warm and cozy and I have everything I need, and it's cold outside, and I'm going to stay here.*

    - *(Right hand) Get up and move!*

- *(Left hand) I want to stay here where it's warm. Why should I get up and move? It's uncomfortable out there.*

    - *(Right hand) I'm feeling paralyzed. I can't stand it.*

Move! Get out of that shell
and move! You're never
going to have anything but
what you've got.
• (Left hand) I've got everything I want.
I'm weary, I'm weary.
It's dull, monotonous.
It's nowhere. But I
don't have the strength
to move. I'm feeling
sorry for myself. I
resent having to move.
I will move. I feel
lighter.

BARBARA
Here are a couple of snatches from a dream.

My two children and I are living with Alvin and Ethel, two
old friends, and their children. We are all living in the same
house. Alvin tries to take a bath, but the bathroom's always
full. My daughter Ann keeps washing things in the bathroom,
which makes for further delay. I lie down on a high bunk-type
bed with their little daughter Sally. I delight in her delicious
feel and warmth and loveliness. I express a sudden insight I
had to Alvin. "Do all people want to be perfect and can't make
it?" His response indicates that's true.

The scene shifts to outside. I see three cucumbers not fully
grown. I think, how great, they can just lie in the sun and
grow into beautiful big cucumbers. The dream ends.

RUTH

I'm jealous. Cucumbers can really be perfect. They don't have to do anything about it. They just lie there in the sun and do it! I have to run all the time and strive to be perfect. They do what they do with no effort at all. It doesn't seem fair.

TOLBERT

I'm going to make it. I've got to get next to people. I don't like it in this crowded house. It's how I'm going to get next to people, that's how a child comes next to me. I can feel people, I can feel youth, I can be young, smooth, delicious, beautiful, crowded, crowded. Outside, free, quiet, slow, slow, ripe, scared. I'm scared of just lying there, letting it happen.

MARSHALL

I'm frustrated. I frustrate myself with questions. Will I be perfect, am I going to be perfect? I am authentic when I am in touch. I like the smell, the taste of touching people. It's delicious. That's what I enjoy. I don't envy the cucumbers. I have what they have.

DONALD

I can feel. Cucumbers can't feel. I don't want to be a cucumber.

TOLBERT

I want to go back to Sally. I want to get away from the profound question. I don't want to have to ask questions, I just want to feel. I want to feel young. I want sex, I want love, I want passion. I want youth.

Ruth

Let's do a thing together. How about a candle fantasy? Close your eyes. You are sitting in a circle. There is a candle in the middle of the circle. At some point get up, go to the center of the circle, pick up the candle and come back to your place.

(Pause as people have and record the fantasy)

Donald

I go out to the center of the circle and get the candle and return and sit down in front of it. A man in a light gray suit on one side of the circle stands up, stands in front of me and gets the candle and returns it to the center. I get up again, get the candle and place it in front of me. Then on the other side of the circle a woman stands up, walks over and gets the candle and returns it to the center. I get up this time and go out to the center, pick up the candle, slam it down and walk out.

Marshall

To hell with it, who needs it! Goodbye.

Tolbert

I do want it. I do want it. I don't want to fight you for it. I'm not going to fight. I'd rather leave than fight.

Ruth

I'm frustrated. God, I'm mad! This is really important to me.

Tolbert

I am sitting in a circle. I go out to the center. There is a very small candle, a votive light. I am disappointed. I always

have big candles in these fantasies! I don't know how to go
with it. I pick up the little light. I'm expecting it to get larger.
It gets smaller. I take it back to my seat and look at the light,
and there is just me and the candle. All the other people fade
away. It's black. It's very black. I am moving very fast and the
candle has moving power. I am holding on to the candle moving through space; way out into space. Beneath me is a blue
planet like earth. I am there with the candle. The candle is
strong. It is beautiful. It is enough.

MARSHALL

I'm disappointed. I expected more fire, more power, more
punch. Then, it's enough; the candle flame is enough. It
does what it has to do. It gives me enough light to see my
way.

RUTH

I always have to get by with less than what I want. Sure I
can make do, but why do I have to do it?

MARSHALL

The candle's small and the flame is the same, the same
amount of light.

TOLBERT

Look down, give me my power. Give in, live, feel, move, go
through, feel the power. Appreciate me, sense me, hold me.

RUTH

We are all sitting in a circle. Some people are standing in
back of the seated group. In the center is a large, multicolored
candle. I am dressed in a flowing, red dress. I pick up the candle

and carry it to each person, then return it to the center of the circle.

TOLBERT

I feel crowded. I'm a spectator. I am galleries. I am crowded, crowded.

BARBARA

I'm not in contact. I try to make contact. It doesn't quite work.

MARSHALL

I don't want to be alone with my candle. I would rather use the candle to minister to other people. My nourishment comes from the way I look to other people. I have no desire to be alone with my candle.

BARBARA

There is a candle in the center of the room. People are sitting around. There is a feeling of togetherness in the room. I go to the center, pick up the candle and walk around with it to greet each person. I feel a little awkward. I find myself wanting to do a dance in and around, weaving in and out. I do, then put the candle in the center and go back to my seat.

TOLBERT

People are looking at me. I have the candle. The people, the people, I can't even appreciate the candle. Maybe if I just dance, the people . . . they'll be all right. What am I supposed to do? I'd better get rid of it, I don't feel comfortable with it. I'll give it away. I'll put it back.

I want the candle! I want the people to get out of here, I want to be with the candle. Me and the candle.

MARSHALL

I go up to the candle, play with the molten wax, blow out the candle, relight it, mold it, take it back to my seat, chew on it, gnaw it, crumble the base, turn it upside down, pull off the molten wax, roll it back to the center.

TOLBERT

Fuss with it, play with it, analyze it, move it, take it apart. It isn't real. Kick it, make it be a candle. I don't believe it. I don't want to be disappointed with this candle. I'll put it on its side, turn it upside down. I'm not going to be still, I'm feeling fast, I'm feeling very fast. Tear apart, destroy, kill.

MARSHALL

I'm not serious; I'm not seeing the candle. I want to rip it apart. I want to fool with it. I don't want to be serious, I want to be light, I want to be vicious. I resent having to see the candle. I resent having to revere it. I resent having to be serious. I want to . . .

RUTH

I don't want the candle. I want to be the light.

TOLBERT

I don't want stillness. I don't want quiet. I don't want to be peaceful. I want light. I want joy. I want to be jumping and flopping. I want connecting.

MARSHALL

I want activity. I don't want the quiet seriousness. I'm afraid of that. I'm afraid of taking it seriously; afraid of taking myself seriously.

RUTH

Be the candle, Marshall.

MARSHALL

I'm being torn apart. I'm being beat up, I'm being abused.
I'm being used in a way that's perverse. It's not what I'm
used for. I'm not being respected. I'm being gnawed and
chewed. I'm being made light of. I'm being ridiculed. I
am helpless. I can't do anything about it. My function is
perverted.

DONALD

I don't want to share my fantasy now. I would like to end
with a quiet thing.

RUTH

Yeah.

TOLBERT

Shall we end with a simple meditation?

BARBARA

That feels very right.

MARSHALL

OK.

(A candle is placed in the center of the room and the group
spends about fifteen minutes in meditation. Each leaves
when it feels right. The last one to leave blows out the
candle and the session ends.)

XI

The Breath of Life

11

SELF-EXPLORATION IS VALUABLE in itself: a way to know what is truly going on with me at a given time. However, I do not have to stop here. The tools in this book can be the basis of a way of life, a means of working on my spiritual growth.

IS IT PSYCHOLOGY?

Are we in the realm of psychology? Psychology has traditionally been concerned mostly with the study of emotional deficiencies. This orientation shows the medical origins of psychiatry in the offices of a number of European physicians. The emotional problems of the patient were attacked in the same fashion as a broken leg: examination, analysis, diagnosis, treatment, and cure.

In the past two decades, a growing number of psychologists have emphasized life's possibilities rather than its problems. In what is often referred to as humanistic psychology, heretical topics have been allowed to pitch a tent on the psychological campground. The statement of purposes of the *Journal of Humanistic Psychology* states that it is a psychology

> concerned with topics having little place in existing theories and systems; e.g., love, creativity, self, growth, organism, basic need gratification, self-actualization, higher values, being, becoming, spontaneity, play, humor, affection, naturalness, warmth, ego transference, objectivity, autonomy, responsibility, meaning, fair play, transcendental experience, peak experience, courage, and related concepts.

Humanistic psychology became a third force standing beside the traditional Freudian view and the extreme behavioristic approach. To this rallying point came many other banners: the Adlerians, Reichians, Jungians, neo-Freudians, advocates of Gestalt theory; and a number of individual champions, such as Gordon Allport, Roberto Assagioli, Hazel Barnes, James Bugental, Rudolf Dreikurs, Erik Erikson, Viktor Frankl, Erich Fromm, Paul Goodman, Sidney Jourard, R. D. Laing, Abraham Maslow, Rollo May, Gardner Murphy, Fritz Perls, Ira Progoff, Carl Rogers, Harry F. Sullivan, Thomas Szasz, and an ever-growing list.

When these various forces coalesced and were given a representative voice, particularly through the writings of Abraham Maslow, there was a great hue and cry from the more traditional psychological community that what these people were focusing on was not psychology. If we define psychology in terms of deficiencies, these objections are undoubtedly correct.

A great deal of energy has been spent in the last twenty years in getting humanistic psychology recognized in the field of psychology. The humanistic psychologists have been successful, and their victory is proving more difficult to handle than a defeat. Now the tendency is to view much of what has been explored by the men mentioned above in a narrow, respectable, academic way, which has caused the early death of so many experiments in living during the past centuries.

Shortly before his death, Maslow put together a second edition of his important work, *Motivation and Personality*. The first edition appeared in 1954. In the preface to the second edition, written sixteen years later, he stated:

However, what I took then to be an argument within the family of psychologists, has in my opinion turned out since then to be rather a local manifestation of the new *zeitgeist,* a new general comprehensive philosophy of life. This new humanistic *Weltanschuung* seems to be a new and far more hopeful and encouraging way of conceiving any and every area of human knowledge: e.g., economics, sociology, biology, and every profession: e.g., law, politics, medicine, and all of the social institutions: e.g., the family, education, religion, etc. I have acted upon this personal conviction in revising this book, writing into the psychology presented herein, the belief that it is an aspect of a much broader world view, and of a comprehensive life philosophy, which is already partly worked out, at least to the point of plausibility, and must, therefore, be taken seriously (1).

In his way Maslow was evidencing the same concern as Chuang Tzu expressed over two thousand years earlier.

From the time of the three dynasties men have been running in all directions. How can they find time to be human?

Some similar thoughts come from an examination of the word "psychology" itself. The Greek goddess Psyche was the goddess of soul or spirit. She personified breath, and more specifically, the breath of life. If psychology is seen as being limited to a study of emotional well-being, then much of what is written here and by humanistic psychologists in not psychology. But if the word is allowed to assume its original meaning, and can break loose from the limitations that now bind it, then, indeed, all that is here and in the writings of the people listed above, and in the writings of all the world's great religious and social teachers, can properly come under the umbrella of the breath of life.

We owe a debt to the emotional technicians who engendered new interest in the humanist approach. But to sense the dimension of this phenomenon we must look with a broader vision to some of man's basic quests: all the old and important questions, including our attempt at religious experience.

Ours is the most religious generation in history. Many people are in quest of a personal spiritual path. However, traditional church programs have become largely irrelevant to these individuals.

A PERSONAL RELIGION

Religion is the process of finding our inner strength. In the quest to give life a personal meaning, or to come in touch with the vital forces of our being, what we believe is unimportant compared to how we live. In commenting on religion in the year 2000, Carl Rogers states:

But religion, to the extent that the term is used, will consist of tentatively held hypotheses which are lived out and corrected in the interpersonal world. Groups, probably much smaller than present-day congregations, will wrestle with the ethical and moral and philosophical questions which are posed by the rapidly changing world. The individual will forge, with the support of the group, the stance he will take in the universe—a stance which he cannot regard as final, because more data will continually be coming in.

In the open questioning and honest struggle to face reality which exists in such a group, it is likely that a sense of true community will develop—a community based not on a common creed nor an unchanging ritual, but on the personalities of individuals who have become deeply related to one another as they attempt to comprehend, and to face as living men, the mysteries of existence. The religion of the future will be man's existential choice of his way of living in an unknown tomorrow—a choice made more bearable because formed in a community of individuals who are like-minded, but like-minded only in their searching (2).

The religion of the future can be seen today in the growing number of individuals who are committing themselves to their own growth. This is a spiritual quest, and goes beyond concern for emotional well-being, conduct, and behavior. The search includes all that one expects to bring to, and to receive from, life.

There has been a tendency in psychology, even humanistic psychology, to avoid the experience itself by taking the safer path of analysis and understanding. Let us look again at the story of Psyche (3). She was a beautiful girl. Her beauty caused jealousy and because of this jealousy she was marked for destruction, but the messenger of her destruction fell in love with her. Her lover was Eros, the God of Love. Psyche was in love with love itself. Nothing could have been more fulfilling, but her jealous sisters urged her not to accept her own feelings and made her suspicious. Did she really know her situation? She had never really seen the face of her lover. She must understand. She must know. She must analyze. She must be able to answer—what and why.

Psyche gave in to the urgings of her sisters and her destruction followed. All that she had prized vanished, and she wandered the world forlorn and alone until she was captured. After her capture she was placed in the hands of two slaves named Anxiety and Grief, who severely punished her. Then she was given impossible tasks to perform. She did perform these tasks, but only because she was assisted again by Eros. Now she knew what was valuable, and sought nothing else but to be reunited with love itself. This union came and Psyche and Eros were wed. Psyche became immortal, and the father of the gods commanded that never again should Eros and Psyche be separated. There is great wisdom in heeding this admonition. Indeed, we need a new prophet to scream this warning in the temples of education, business, government, religion, and even in the antitemple of revolution.

Laurens van der Post found his prophet living on the Kalahari Desert.

... I would use what knowledge I had of the Bushman, his mind and way of life in the desert, merely to interpret the experience into a contemporary idiom and so try to make it accessible to the modern imagination. That, however amateurish or small, could be the beginning of better things, because what the world lacks today is not so much knowledge of these first things as experience of them.

We know so much intellectually, indeed, that we are in danger of becoming the prisoners of our knowledge. We suffer from a hubris of the mind. We have abolished superstition of the heart only to install a superstition of the intellect in its place. We behave as if there were some magic in mere thought, and we use thinking for purposes for which it was never designed. As a result we are no longer sufficiently aware of the importance of what we cannot know intellectually, what we must know in other ways, of the living experience before and beyond our transitory knowledge. The passion of the spirit, which would inspire man to live his finest hour dangerously on the exposed frontier of his knowledge, seemed to me to have declined into a vague and arid restlessness hiding behind an arrogant intellectualism, as a child of arrested development behind the skirts of its mother.

Intellectually, modern man knows almost all there is to know about the pattern of creation in himself, the forms it takes, the surface designs it describes. He has measured the pitch of its rhythms and carefully recorded all the mechanics. From the outside he sees the desirable first object of life more clearly perhaps than man has ever seen it before. But less and less does he experience the process within. Less and less is he capable of committing himself body and soul to the creative experiment that is continually seeking to fire him and to charge his little life with great objective meaning. Cut off by accumulated knowledge from the heart of his own living experience, he moves among a comfortable rubble of material possessions, alone and unbelonging, sick, poor, starved of meaning. How different the naked little Bushman, who could carry all he possessed in one hand! Whatever his life lacked, I never felt that it was meaning. Meaning for him died only when we bent him to our bright twentieth-century will. Otherwise, he was rich where we were poor; he walked clear-cut through my mind, clothed in his own vivid experience of the dream of life within him. By comparison most of the people I saw on my way to the sea were blurred, and like the knight at arms in Keats' frightening allegory, "palely loitering" through life (4).

However the phenomenon is characterized, as religion, a way of life, or simply as life, it can only be fully comprehended as an experience. There is a limit to how far a person can go without a commitment to his own growth and an acceptance of a self-discipline that goes beyond an attempt at self-understanding.

FREEDOM AND COMMITMENT

Commitment and discipline are strange words in the age of freedom. Everything in modern times has stressed that man must be free from the fetters in which he has bound himself. We have legitimately focused on the process of freedom.

But freedom is negative and relative. We are attempting to become free from something. In a speech given in 1964, Carl Rogers said:

In the first place, the freedom that I am talking about is essentially an inner thing, something which exists in the living person quite aside from any of the outward choices of alternatives which we so often think of as constituting freedom. I am speaking of the kind of freedom which Viktor Frankl vividly describes in his experience of the concentration camp, when everything—possessions, identity, choice—was taken from the prisoners. But even months and years in such an environment showed only "that everything can be taken from a man but one thing: the last of the human freedoms—to choose one's own attitude in any given set of circumstances, to choose one's own way." It is this inner, subjective, existential freedom which I have observed. It is the realization that "I can live myself, here and now, by my own choice." It is the quality of courage which enables a person to step into the uncertainty of the unknown as he chooses himself. It is the discovery of meaning from within oneself, meaning which comes from listening sensitively and openly to the complexities of what one is experiencing. It is the burden of being responsible for the self one chooses to be. It is the recognition of a person that he is an emerging process, not a static end product. The individual who is thus deeply and courageously thinking his own thoughts, becoming his own uniqueness, responsibly choosing himself, may be fortunate in having hundreds of objective outer alternatives from which to choose, or he may be unfortunate in having none. But his freedom exists regardless. So we are first of all speaking of something which exists within the individual, something phenomenological rather than objective, but nonetheless to be prized (5).

Both freedom and commitment are something that you discover in yourself. They are the acceptance of decisions already made. Freedom is freedom to make a choice. A growing number of young people today are not satisfied with reliving details of the great battles by which man found freedom. They have not experienced as much bondage as some of us who propose to be their teachers. In my college days many teachers I admired seemed to be characterized by a tendency toward critique for critique's sake. I could never quite verbalize my objection to this. Somehow I was not receiving what I wanted most from them; their dreams, their risk, their own commitment. Today's young people find the same lack in us as we seek freedom for freedom's sake. Indeed, many who hold positions in our universities and colleges have become proficient in an elaborate game of judging every dream and knocking down everything, while they never risk anything and never put out any type of positive statement that can be judged by others. Neither more critique nor more freedom is what is needed at this time. In order to go forward, it is necessary to have commitment, and commitments are risky. They mean moving without guarantees. Our young people demand that all of us risk, that we experiment, that we quit talking about what is not possible and focus on what is possible.

The removal of personal commitment, the removal of Eros from the study of life, has led to a respectable but cold scientific view that now has become a new orthodoxy. Michael Polanyi said:

> In the days when an idea could be silenced by showing that it was contrary to religion, theology was the greatest single source of fallacies. Today, when any human thought can be discredited by branding it as unscientific, the power previously exercised by theology has passed over to science; hence science has become in its turn the greatest single source of error (6).

There is also a danger from the professors and writers who watch the commitment and growth of spiritual men in order that they might dazzle their students with a half blind account of where those young people hope to go. The constant question is, will the professor stand aside when the student is ready to go beyond him?

Once Jesus challenged the jurists. These men had knowledge of the spiritual law, the steps by which people could travel to fulfillment. What he said to them could be repeated today to all in the field of human development and growth.

Woe to you . . . [who] have taken the key that unlocks
the door of knowledge. You have not entered yourselves
and you have stopped those who were entering (7).

LIVING WITH UNCERTAINTY

As a race we have been hurt, and now we do not want to
risk. Somehow we must find the encouragement to risk, and
by risking free the great creative energy within us. We must
learn to live with uncertainty; to quit trying to distinguish
between what is certain and uncertain. It was our natural
condition in the caves. Living in such a situation calls forth
our strength and our vitality. The demand for, and worse yet
the finding of, a supposed security, heralds our destruction.
"Every moment of life," says the poet Robert Duncan, "is
an attempt to come to life." We must again learn to live on
our own frontiers. In moments of crisis men often go in
search of certainty, be it the certainty of a god, a devil, a
spirit, a science, an institution, or a theory. Whatever a
person's certainty, he will find evidence to support it. Yet,
our salvation lies in an opposite direction. Maurice Friedman
believes that "today meaning can be found, if at all, only
through the attitude of the man who is willing to *live* with
the absurd, to remain open to the mystery which he can
never hope to pin down" (8).

Our academic cynicism is but a thin veil hiding our fear
of being hurt. We strive in every way possible to find a
position of aloofness, a position out of contact with other
men, and yet our true happiness lies in the simple interaction
necessary to form a community of men. Some years ago a
poet died in San Francisco following a long, agonizing ill-

ness, during which he regained consciousness, looked around the room at his friends, and said, "For the past ten years I have been suffering under the wrong vocabulary. To those I could have loved, I am sorry." While there is still life in us, let us get out from under the wrong vocabulary, and again commit ourselves to risk, to clumsiness, to error, and above all to life. I can rejoin Eros and Psyche in me. Such a union makes me vulnerable, but it is only the vulnerable man who lives.

XII

Spiritual Growth

TOOLS OF SELF-EXPLORATION can be important steps in traveling a daily path in which we attempt to come into contact with our own inner strength. These tools can put us in touch with a great teacher within, who demands of us a discipline no less strenuous than that of any disciple of any religious leader throughout history.

In this journey we are susceptible to all kinds of self-trickery. But the company of others on the same quest or the writings of those who have undertaken this route provide guidance. "A blind man," says St. John of the Cross, "if he be not quite blind, refuses to be led by a guide; and since he sees a little he thinks it better to go in whatever happens to be the direction which he can distinguish, because he sees none better; and thus he can lead astray a guide who sees more than he, for after all, it is for him to say where he shall go, rather than for the guide" (1).

St. John also warns us that daily discipline is like a bird. Once you have let it out of your hand you will never recapture it. Perhaps you will find another bird sometime, but never the one you let fly away.

Your individual path of spiritual enlightenment can be assisted by a commitment to explore your inner world in the manner suggested in this book. A thorough discussion of the path of spiritual development would lead us into dimensions beyond the scope of this book; it is the task for another time. What follows is an attempt to open the door briefly on this rich area of human experience.

GOING HOME

The most important step on the spiritual path is the

decision to stop moving in our present direction. This is a basic and simple idea, but one that is often difficult to grasp. We do not listen. We are casual. Even our humor is often a way of avoiding investing in ourselves. Most of life is spent in frantically adding on. We collect tricks and short-cuts to momentarily take our attention away from the deep pain we feel. We have lost our way and we do not admit it. We do not want to hear the loneliness, so we pass on, adding more things and burdens and self-deceptions.

What follows are many different ways of saying the same thing. Perhaps one of these will have a personal meaning for you.

• In the thirteenth century Meister Eckhart advised his spiritual followers:

> People look in vain for peace, who seek it in the world outside, in places, people, ways, activities, or in the world-flight, poverty, and humiliation, whatever the avenue or degree; for there is no peace this way. They are looking in the wrong direction, and the longer they look the less they find what they are looking for. They go along like someone who has missed the road; the farther they go the more they are astray (2).

• There are many gnostic references similar to the cabalistic Tree of Life. These teach that we come from a simple unified existence. We were catapulted to the outer limb of a tree. Most of us will crawl to higher limbs or look out into space. A few will do neither of these things. There is in each of us a tiny spark. We brought this spark with us from our former home. A few of us will remain still, listen to this spark, and then turn and go back down the tree into the roots. There are many important moments on that backward journey. One of the most difficult is the moment in which we really have it all together and we begin to see the whole picture. We are feeling strong and contented. Do we bask in our own good fortune and troop our talents before those less aware? The more fulfilling alternative is to let go of even these accomplishments and surrender to the strong pull toward the process of continued simplicity and close unity with the basic forces of life.

• The Sufi poet Farid ud-Din Attar wrote of birds who had long ago been separated from their homeland (3). In his fable the birds are encouraged to journey to the palace of the great Simurgh. Each bird wanted to go, yet had some excuse for staying where he was. At last they set out and the journey was difficult. Thousands of birds fell by the wayside, destroyed by the elements, fatigue, hunger, thirst, discouragement, fighting, greed, and a host of other problems. At the end only thirty birds remained. They were half dead when they came to worship at the Simurgh's palace. Here they found their home. They also discovered that the Simurgh was but a mirror to help them find the divinity within themselves. So they stopped worshiping the mirror and became the Simurgh. A peaceful new life began for them.

• The Buddhist speaks of the stopping as "awakening." "Awake and Sing" says the Bible. The African Bushman says "There is a dream dreaming me." What if all this is a dream?

Imagine that all this around you, your troubles and joys, all your accomplishments and failures, all these things are a dream.

Now, imagine that you wake up. Where are you? How are you? Who are you?

• Hermann Hesse told us to value our sense of home-sickness as our greatest asset. The Taoist attempts to move in a "backward flowing motion." Many have suggested that the most fulfilling life is the one that helps us arrive back at the place from which we started and to know that place for the first time.

• Each of us leaves home and goes on a journey. As we get farther and farther away we begin to drift and become dull. We forget where we came from. We play with unimportant toys along the way. Every moment takes us farther away.

Lao Tzu has some practical advice on going home in chapter sixteen of the *Tao Te Ching*. He urges us to watch nature. A flower comes out of the union between the seed, the soil, and water. The flower blooms and dies. Then it rots away and returns its elements to the earth. The earth remains forever. Sometimes it shuffles itself into plants and sometimes it just remains as it is. We are overly concerned about our individual destiny. We use our cleverness to make things happen. Lao Tzu asks us:

> Can you make a muddy pool become clear?
> Be still and the mud will settle.

When a river comes over a cliff, a waterfall results. Every falling drop seems completely alone and individual. Then they all drop into the pool at the bottom of the waterfall. There is stillness.

THE TAO TE CHING, CHAPTER 16

1 Empty everything out
  and be at peace.

All things around us rise and fall.
We can watch all the parts of nature
return to their roots.

Silently returning to the root
is the way in which all things
complete their mission and
report back to their source.

2   Nature never changes.
Knowing the unchanging ways
brings understanding.
Not knowing leads to franticness.

Understanding nature
can help keep your mind open.

An open mind can lead to
a feeling of unity with all things,
and this leads to a royal character.

With this royal character
you can learn heavenly ways
and put your feet upon the great path.

He who is on the path
endures for a long time.
For even though the body dies
the great path continues.

Some may take the opportunity to slow down, to listen
to the voice of homesickness, to stop. The road home requires an initial awakening and then a turning around. Once
we turn and start back there are a number of steps. The
medieval mystics talked about purgation, illumination, and
unity. We start by ridding ourselves of the games we play

and some of the values we have held. Then we learn to listen, to become truly and deeply aware of all that we experience. We must gain a new perspective on life. It is here that we must listen carefully to the teacher within us. We journey to the inner world to bring unity between our outer and inner experiences. Here we leave the preoccupation with maintaining the mask of selfhood and give up the manipulative arts we have learned. At this point we begin to flow in organic partnership with all that is around us.

Each man must write of his own voyage to his home. The purpose of this book has been to encourage some to set forth on that journey. The process of writing the book has been a step in my own journey, a journey to the center where there will no longer be a difference between the inner and the outer.

NOTES AND REFERENCES

Chapter I: THE EXPEDITION AND THE EQUIPMENT

1. Horney, Karen. *Our Inner Conflicts*. New York: W. W. Norton, 1945.
2. Laing, R. D. *The Politics of Experience*. London: 1967. Copyright © R. D. Laing, 1967. Reprinted by permission of Penguin Books Ltd.
3. Jung, Carl G. *Memories, Dreams, Reflections*, recorded and edited by Aniela Jaffé, trans. by Richard and Clara Winston. Copyright © 1961, 1962, 1963 by Random House, Inc. Reprinted by permission of Pantheon Books, a division of Random House, Inc.
4. Merton, Thomas. *The Climate of Monastic Prayer*. Spencer, Mass.: Cistercian Publications, 1969. Reprinted with permission of the publisher.
5. Blakely, Raymond B., trans. *Meister Eckhart*. New York: Harper & Row, 1941. Reprinted with permission of the publisher.
6. St. John of the Cross. *Poems*. Trans. by Roy Campbell. London: Penguin Books, 1951.
7. Blake, William. *The Poetry and Prose of William Blake*. David V. Erdmann, ed. New York: Doubleday, 1970.
8. Neihardt, John G. *Black Elk Speaks*. Lincoln, Nebraska: University of Nebraska Press, 1961.
9. Trungpa, Chogyam. *Meditation in Action*. Berkeley: Shambala, 1970. Reprinted with permission of the publisher.

Chapter II: THE JOURNAL

1. Among the approaches to journals emphasizing psychological understanding are the suggestions of Ira Progoff in his Intensive Journal Workshops. A major modification on Progoff's methods is contained in a helpful paper by Gordon Tappan of California State College, Sonoma, "Notes on Journal Keeping" (1971).
2. Thoreau, Henry David. *Journals of Henry D. Thoreau*. New York: Dover, 1906.
3. Most of what is in this and all the following chapters is based on my experience as a facilitator in the Me Groups at the Humanist Institute (1430 Masonic Avenue, San Francisco, California 94117). These intensive self-exploration groups use the tools mentioned in

this book. More information on these groups is contained in chapters IX and X.

4. From *An Introduction to Haiku* by Harold G. Henderson. Copyright © 1958 by Harold G. Henderson. Reprinted by permission of Doubleday and Company, Inc.
5. Proverbs 5:15.
6. A few weeks before publication of the book I received a copy of some comments of a sensitive woman who teaches psychology at California State College, Sonoma. She is also a well-known educational consultant and workshop leader. Like so many of us who help other people grow, she forgot about herself at times—until she met her journal. Her comments were headed: "Journal Keeping—A Gift to Me."

I have dibbled and dabbled in diaries, journals, autobiographical statements since I was twelve years old. I began keeping a daily journal, of the kind I keep now, on January 7, 1970. Connections I make around what started me in this venture are: a New Year's party seven days earlier at which someone asked me rather loosely at 2 A.M., "And what is this year going to be for you?" To which I responded rather solemnly, "I think this year will be the first in my life as a woman-mother where I will be able to say 'me first' as I did between my nineteenth and twenty-seventh year of life." I had had good practicing years and had not lost touch with that part of myself; I had relinquished to the needs of life temporarily, for twelve years.

January 2 I received a brochure in the mail announcing a "Me Group" and decided that that must be where one learns to say "me first" again. I joined the group and . . . what I learned . . . in terms of journal-keeping techniques, as well as honesty and integrity, I will never forget. Before, I had available to me all the techniques of my colleagues [in the Psychology Department], but my weekly trips to San Francisco to be with these groups for thirty weeks, and the commitment I made to myself at that time, were really what allowed the venture into my inner world to become a deep, ongoing, disciplined, and loving experience. I became more committed to that part of myself which feels that "Life is a mystery to be lived, not a problem to be solved."

The form of the journal changes with practice, but what I do consistently is:

In the morning I record my dreams, or feelings, or sensings about what the night said to me. In the evening I log my day, always. Then I work in an art form—collage, doodle, or mandala—almost always: art as an impression—another "this is me" experience. Then I move in whatever direction this takes me—fantasy dream extensions, dialogues, meditation, tracking of dream series or of emotions. I need to continually push my own limits and find my new perimeters . . .

The function of the journal has grown in terms of depth of experience for me. It continues to tell me about commitment to myself—I have missed writing in it 5 days in 3 years and am now unable to sleep if I do not write—but I experience the changes mostly in my relationship to others: the openness and lack of confusion I feel, even when under pressure, is a function of the journal I had not anticipated. Anger, frustration, unfinished business are dealt with daily in my writing; very few negative or non-constructive emotions hang on.

I remember talking with a fellow journal keeper about the journal as an "enemy" after keeping one for about six months. What I had become aware of then was that my journal literally would not tolerate lies—even if I wrote something that was a half-truth I would become very uncomfortable; even if it was not intentional, if I was hiding from myself, it seemed that the moment I was writing in the journal I would become wary of what I was saying and feel the discomfort in my body. Of course there are things I do not know or am unaware of—but those are not the things that make me uncomfortable. It is impossible to think of what one does not know.

In a very deep sense giving up some sort of dignity vis-a-vis myself, allowing myself to go wherever my thoughts and feelings took me, at least in my journal, has allowed me to become my own best friend. Me and the journal, the journal and I—the relationship I have that is as honest as I know how and in which I feel good and whole—good even when what we are dealing with is ugly, despicable, or crazy.

I have also made important connections with the spiritual part of me, which seems to be a synthesis between the religious, philosophical, psychological, and ordinary me. I have learned to sense the relatedness of all parts of me in dreams, acts, thoughts, attitudes, values. I am aware of diversity and unification and of my daily need for centering.

The journal is also preventative inasmuch as I can only go into tomorrow if I have cleared today—it prevents pile-up, overreaction, inappropriate action. And it is educational, of course, and very therapeutic and a great deal of fun. It gives me a sense of proportion and helps keep my life balanced—if I become very adult the child in me will laugh. Counterpoint. I know when the music is flat.

Beyond what I know at a conscious level, I feel a unification that is taking place in me I do not yet understand, which I cherish with gratefulness and something of a sense of humility, and for which I have very few words.

Chapter III: INNER IMAGERY

1. These fantasies were selected from the journals of Marti McCurdie and myself. For us this particular fantasy usually helps focus on individual situations and is a good yardstick for discovering how congruent our lives are with our desires, or actual feelings. For others the wall fantasy helps bring more basic or long range issues into focus.
2. All these structures have been used extensively in groups at the Humanist Institute. A number of them originated in sessions conducted by Gordon Tappan at California State College, Sonoma. Some are adaptations of structures from older sources.
3. Not infrequently, when a group of people do a fantasy at the same time, persons sitting next to each other will have the same symbols in their fantasies. Although this is an interesting phenomenon, it does not have any bearing on the individual's message from his inner world. The use of the symbol varies greatly between the individuals involved.

Chapter IV: DREAMS

1. Aserinsky, E. and Kleitman, N. "Regularly Occurring Periods of Eye Mobility and Concomitant Phenomena During Sleep." *Science*, 1953, 118, pp. 273–274.
2. Oswald, Ian. *Sleep*. Baltimore: Penguin, 1966, p. 72.
3. Hartmann, E. L. "The D-State: A Review and Discussion on the Physiological State Concomitant with Dreaming." *International Journal of Psychiatry*, 1966, 2, pp. 11–31.
4. Freud, Sigmund. *The Interpretation of Dreams*. New York: Basic Books, 1955.
5. Adler, Alfred. *Superiority and Social Interest*. Heinz and Rowena Ansbacher, eds. Evanston, Illinois: Northwestern University Press, 1964.
6. Jung, Carl G., ed. *Man and His Symbols*. Garden City, New York: Doubleday & Company, 1964.
7. Perls, Fredrick S. *Gestalt Therapy Verbatim*. Lafayette, California: Real People Press, 1969.
8. Stewart, Kilton. "Culture and Personality in Two Primitive Groups," *Complex*, Winter 1953–1954, p. 20.

9. Stewart, Kilton. "Dream Theory in Malaya" in Charles Tart, ed. *Altered States of Consciousness*. New York: John Wiley & Sons, 1969.

10. Oswald. *Sleep*, pp. 81–82.

11. Hartmann, E. L. "The D-State: A Review and Discussion of Studies on the Physiologic State Concomitant with Dreaming." *New England Journal of Medicine*, 1965, 273, pp. 30–35, 87–92.

12. For many people different types of dreams are associated with specific times in their sleep cycle. After learning from a native American psychic that in her culture, prophetic dreams were frequently morning dreams, I began looking at the timing of my dreams and those of my associates. A casual investigation turned up some interesting things. For several of us the following pattern evolved. In the early stages of sleep our dreams were more likely to help us see what was really going on with us. What had we been hiding? What did we truly want? In the deep sleep of the middle of the night there was less self and problems in our dreams. Here we could come in touch with the basic parts of our story. In the dreams of early morning, either it was easier to hear the clues as to what we should do, or the dreams would provide an overview of our lives. At times the morning dreams projected our present conduct into the future and predicted what was to come.

13. Some people have the feeling that there is only one dream that they have in their whole life. The dream is going on all the time. During the waking hours the dream is difficult or impossible to hear, but the experience continues. On his deathbed a young friend talked to me with joy about now living only in the dream world. The Bushmen have that fascinating saying mentioned in chapter XII, "There is a dream dreaming me."

14. The early Christian desert fathers were interested in dreams. This is particularly reflected in the writings of Evagrius Ponticus (345–399 AD). Evagrius was a brilliant Byzantine scholar who left urban life to live as a hermit in Egypt. There he was formed in the simple Coptic traditions of desert spirituality. Dom John Eudes Bamberger (a Cistercian Abbot who was trained as a psychiatrist) observes, "Evagrius had a remarkable knowledge of dream-psychology which presents many points of comparison with modern dynamic theories and observations." See Evagrius Ponticus, *The Praktikos, Chapters on Prayer*. Translated, with an introduction and notes, by

John Eudes Bamberger, O.C.S.O. Spenser, Mass.: Cistercian Publications, 1970.

Chapter V: ART EXPERIENCES

1. For a general explanation of the relation of art to growth in terms of Gestalt therapy, see Janie Rhyne, *The Gestalt Art Experience*. Monterey, California: Brooks/Cole, 1973.
2. Argüelles, José and Miriam. *Mandala*. Berkeley: Shambala, 1972.
3. Jung, Carl G. *Memories, Dreams, Reflections*. Recorded and edited by Aniela Jaffé, trans. by Richard and Clara Winston. Copyright © 1961, 1962, 1963, by Random House, Inc. Reprinted by permission of Pantheon Books, a division of Random House, Inc.
4. *Ibid.*
5. Schopenhauer, Arthur. *Art of Literature*. Ann Arbor: Univ. of Michigan Press, 1960.

Chapter VI: MEDITATION

1. Feng, Gia-Fu and Kirk, Jerome. *Tai Chi—a Way of Centering and I Ching*. London: Collier Books, 1970.
2. Vishnudevananda, Swami. *The Complete Illustrated Book of Yoga*. New York: Bell-Crown, 1960.
3. For a simple and interesting account of the spiritual development of a Russian pilgrim who followed the Hesychast method read *The Way of a Pilgrim*. New York: The Seabury Press, 1965.
4. Happold, F. C. *Mysticism, A Study and an Anthology*. Baltimore: Penguin Books, 1960.
5. Sitting for spiritual exercises is not an exclusively Oriental practice. The following words are from Richard Rolle, a fourteenth-century mystic of northern England.

   "I have loved to sit . . . because I knew I loved God more and lasted longer within the comfort of love, than going, or standing, or kneeling. For by sitting am I in most rest, and my heart most upward."

6. Trungpa, Chogyam. *Meditation in Action*. Berkeley: Shambala, 1970.
7. Suzuki, Shunryu. *Zen Mind, Beginner's Mind*. New York: Weatherhill, 1970.

Chapter VII: FROM THE OCCULT

1. Jung, Carl G. *Man and His Symbols.* Copyright © 1964, Aldus Books, London. Reprinted with permission of the publisher.
2. van der Post, Laurens. *The Heart of the Hunter.* New York: William Morrow, 1961.
   ———. *The Lost World of the Kalahari.* New York: William Morrow, 1958.
3. *The Collected Works of C. G. Jung.* Edited by G. Adler, M. Fordham, and H. Read. Translated by R. F. C. Hull. Bollingen Series XX, vol. 12, *Psychology and Alchemy* (Copyright © 1953 and 1968 by Bollingen Foundation), reprinted by permission of Princeton University Press.
4. Papus (Encausse, Gerard). *The Tarot of the Bohemians.* A. P. Morton, trans. New York: Samuel Weiser, 1958.
5. Cavendish, Richard. *The Black Arts.* New York: Capricorn Books, 1967, Chapter 3.
6. Wilhelm, Richard, trans. *The I Ching.* English translation by Cary F. Baynes. Princeton, New Jersey: Princeton University Press, 1967, 3rd ed.
7. Feng, Gia-Fu and Kirk, Jerome. *Tai Chi—A Way of Centering and I Ching.* London: Collier Books, 1970.

Chapter VIII: MORE TOOLS

1. Lowen, Alexander. *Betrayal of the Body.* New York: Macmillan, 1966.
2. Wright, Erna. *The New Childbirth.* New York: Hart Publishing Company, 1966.
3. Feng, Gia-Fu and Kirk, Jerome. *Tai Chi—A Way of Centering and I Ching.* London: Collier Books, 1970.
4. Assagioli, Roberto. *Psychosynthesis: A Manual of Principles and Techniques.* New York: Hobbs, Dorman, 1965. Reprinted with permission of the publisher.
5. Huxley, Laura. *You Are Not the Target.* Copyright © 1963 by Laura Huxley. New York: Farrar, Straus & Giroux, Inc., 1963. Quoted with consent of the publisher.

Chapter X: A SESSION

1. This transcript was made in the early years of the Me Group's' evolution. Today the experience is far more intensive. I used this older model because I felt it would more likely parallel the experiences in a newly formed group.

Chapter XI: THE BREATH OF LIFE

1. Maslow, Abraham. *Motivation and Personality.* 2nd edition. New York: Harper & Row, 1970. Reprinted with permission of the publisher.
2. Rogers, Carl. "Interpersonal Relations: U.S. 2000." *Journal of Applied Behavioral Science,* Vol. 4, No. 3, 1968. Reprinted with permission of the *Journal of Applied Behavioral Science.*
3. *The Golden Ass of Apuleius.* Robert Graves, trans. New York: Farrar, Straus and Giroux, 1951.
4. van der Post, Laurens. *The Heart of the Hunter.* Copyright © 1961 by Laurens van der Post. New York: William Morrow, 1961. Reprinted with permission of the publisher.
5. Rogers, Carl. "Freedom and Commitment." An address, March 14, 1964, Washington, D.C. Copyright © by Carl Rogers 1964. Reprinted with permission of the author.
6. Polanyi, Michael. "Scientific Outlook: Its Sickness and Cure." *Science,* Vol. 125, 480–484, 15 March 1957. Reprinted with permission of *Science* and the author.
7. Luke 11:52.
8. Friedman, Maurice. *The Problematic Rebel.* New York: Random House, 1963.

Chapter XII: SPIRITUAL GROWTH

1. Peers, E. Allison, ed. *The Complete Works of Saint John of the Cross.* Vol. 1. Westminster, Md.: The Newman Press, 1951.
2. Blakney, Raymond B., trans. *Meister Eckhart.* New York: Harper & Row, 1941. Reprinted with permission of the publisher.
3. Attar, Farid ud-Din. *The Conference of the Birds.* Trans. by C. S. Nott from the French translation of Garcin de Tassy. Berkeley: Shambala, 1971.

SUGGESTED READINGS

Among the helpful suggestions received from Arthur Ceppos of The Julian Press was the recommendation for a list of books for additional reading. It would not be feasible to assemble a complete list of books relating to spiritual and personal growth. To some extent almost every book is a part of an author's development and can teach us something. So where to begin? The task seemed overpowering when I was attempting to compile THE list of books. However, it became a joyful process when I decided to put together MY list of books.

I. STEPPINGSTONES. Each of us is on a path. We often wander from one side of the road to the other, but basically we keep going ahead. Sometimes we move fast, sometimes more slowly. If we stop and look back, we can see events and people who have been in the main channel of our travels. This process can be an enriching tool for self-exploration. Imagine books and authors as steppingstones. Write down the ones that were the most directly relevant to where you are now. You may be surprised at what comes. Do not try to look proper. Make your list and then read mine.

In most cases the more recent publications are mentioned in the list below. Often these are the paperback editions.

SPIRITUAL GROWTH

India

Bhagavad Gita As It Is. Trans. and commentary by Swami A. C. Bhaktivedanta. Collier.

Tagore, Rabindranath. *The Religion of Man*. Beacon.

Vishnudevananda, Swami. *The Complete Illustrated Book of Yoga*. Bell-Crown.

China

Tao Te Ching. Gia-Fu Feng and Jane English, trans. Vintage.
I Ching. Richard Wilhelm and Cary F. Baynes, trans., commentary by C. G. Jung. Princeton University.
Secret of the Golden Flower. Richard Wilhelm and Cary F. Baynes, trans., commentary by C. G. Jung. Harcourt, Brace & World.
Mai-Maisze. *The Tao of Painting.* Princeton University.
The Texts of Taoism. James Legge, trans. Dover.
The Way of Chuang Tzu. Thomas Merton, trans. New Directions.

Japan

Bashō, Matsu. *Narrow Road to the Deep North.* Penguin.
*Henderson, H. G., *An Introduction to Haiku.* Doubleday.
Issa. *The Year of My Life.* University of California.
*Suzuki, Shunryu. *Zen Mind, Beginner's Mind.* John Weatherhill.

Tibet

Trungpa, Chogyam. *Born in Tibet.* Penguin.
*   *Meditation in Action.* Shambala.
        Cutting Through Spiritual Materialism. Shambala.

Desert

St. Athanasius. *Life of St. Anthony.* Robert Meyer, trans. Ancient Christian Writers Series. Newman Press.
Attar, Farid ud-Din. *The Conference of the Birds.* C. S. Mott, trans. Shambala.
The Bible. James Moffatt, trans. Harper.
*Ponticus, Evagrius. *The Praktikos, Chapters on Prayer.* Cistercian Publications.
Merton, Thomas. *Climate of Monastic Prayer.* Cistercian Publications.
        Mystics and Zen Masters. Delta.
        Spiritual Direction and Meditation. Liturgical Press.
        The Wisdom of the Desert. A translation of the "Verba Seniorum." New Directions.
Palladius, Lausiac History. Robert Meyer, trans. Ancient Christian Writers Series. Newman Press.

Idries Shah, *The Sufis*. Doubleday.
The Gospel According to Thomas. A. Guillaumont, trans. Harper &
Row.
Laurens van der Post, *The Lost World of the Kalahari*. Apollo.
The Heart of the Hunter. Apollo.
*Western Asceticism. Owen Chadwick, ed. A translation of the
"Verba Seniorum," selections from Cassian's "Conferences,"
and the Rule of St. Benedict. The Westminster Press.
Waddell, Helen. *Desert Fathers*. University of Michigan Press.

Native American
Castaneda, Carlos. *The Teachings of Don Juan: A Yaqui Way of
Knowledge*. University of California.
A Separate Reality. Pocket Books.
Journey to Ixtlan. Simon & Schuster.
Neihardt, John C. *Black Elk Speaks*. University of Nebraska.
Nequatewa, Edmund. *Truth of a Hopi*. Museum of Northern Ari-
zona.
Villasenor, David. *Tapestries in Sand*. Naturegraph.
Waters, Frank (with White Bear). *Book of the Hopi*. Ballantine.
Willoya, William and Brown, Vinson. *Warriors of the Rainbow*.
Naturegraph.

Western
Andrews, Edward D. *The People Called Shakers*. Dover.
The Gift to be Simple. Dover.
St. Bernard. *On the Song of Songs*. Cistercian Publications.
Cloud of Unknowing. Clifton Wolters, trans. Penguin.
*Meister Eckhart. R. B. Blakney, trans. Harper.
Epictetus. *Enchiridion*. Liberal Arts Press.
The Hymn of the Robe of Glory. Contained in C. R. S. Mead,
Echoes from the Gnosis. Theosophical Publishing Society.
**Happold, F. C. *Mysticism: A Study and Anthology* Penguin.
Rolle, Richard. *Fire of Love*. Clifton Wolters, trans. Penguin.
The Way of a Pilgrim. The Seabury Press.
William of St. Thierry. *The Golden Epistle*. Cistercian Publications.

Spanish
The Complete Works of Saint John of the Cross. Ed. by E. Allison
   Peers. Newman Press.
St. John of the Cross: Poems. Roy Campbell, trans. Penguin.
St. Teresa of Avila. The Way of Perfection. Doubleday.

WESTERN LITERATURE

The Poetry and Prose of William Blake. Doubleday.
Camus, Albert. *Exile and the Kingdom.* Vintage.
   Resistance, Rebellion and Death. Modern Library.
   The Plague. Modern Library.
   The Fall. Vintage.
   Notebooks, 2 vols. Alfred Knopf.
Duncan, Robert. *The Opening of the Field.* Grove.
   Roots and Branches. Scribners.
Eliot, T. S. *Four Quartets.* Harcourt, Brace.
Hesse, Hermann. *Peter Camenzind.* Noonday.
   Beneath the Wheel. Noonday.
   Demian. Bantam.
*   *Wandering.* Noonday.
*   *Narcissus and Goldmund.* Noonday.
   Journey to the East. Noonday.
*   *Siddhartha.* New Directions.
Williams, William Carlos. *Selected Poems.* New Directions.

PSYCHOLOGY AND SCIENCE

Adler, Alfred. *Individual Psychology of Alfred Adler.* H. R. Ans-
   bacher and R. R. Ansbacher, eds. Harper.
Bugental, J. F. T. *Search for Authenticity.* Rinehart, Winston.
de Chardin, Teilhard. *The Phenomenon of Man.* Harper.
Dreikurs, Rudolf. *Children: The Challenge.* With Vicki Soltz.
   Hawthorne.
   Social Equality: The Challenge of Today. Regnery.
Jung, Carl G. *Memories, Dreams, and Reflections.* Random House.
   Collected Works. Bollingen Series, Princeton University.

Maslow, Abraham H. *Toward a Psychology of Being.* Van Nostrand.
   Religions, Values and Peak Experiences. Viking.
   Motivation and Personality, 2nd ed. Harper.
Perls, Fritz, with Goodman and Hefferline. *Gestalt Therapy.* Julian
   Press.
   Gestalt Therapy Verbatim. Real People.
   In and Out of the Garbage Pail. Real People.
Piaget, Jean. *Language and Thought of a Child.* Humanities.
Polanyi, Michael. *The Study of Man.* University of Chicago.
Rogers, Carl. *On Becoming a Person.* Houghton-Mifflin.
   Person to Person. With Barry Stevens. Real People.
Rhyne, Janie. *The Gestalt Art Experience.* Brooks/Cole.

ADVENTURE

Bach, Richard. *Jonathan Livingston Seagull.* Macmillan.
Baum, Frank. *The Oz Books.* 14 vols. Reilly & Lee Co.
Duncan, Robert. *The Cat and the Blackbird.* White Rabbit.
Milne, A. A. *Winnie the Pooh.* Dutton.
   The House at Pooh Corner. Dutton.
de Saint Exupéry, Antoine. *The Little Prince.* Harcourt, Brace &
   World.
Tolkein, J. R. R. *The Hobbit.* Ballantine.
   The Lord of the Rings. 3 vols. Ballantine.
Wilder, Laura Ingalls. *Little House in the Big Woods.* Harper.
   Little House on the Prairie. Harper.
   Farmer Boy. Harper.
   On the Banks of Plum Creek. Harper.
   By the Shores of Silver Lake. Harper.
   The Long Winter. Harper.
   The Little Town on the Prairie. Harper.
Wright, Austin Tappan. *Islandia.* New American Library.

II. SPECIAL BOOKS. There are some books that continue to be
steppingstones over and over again. These are books that we
never want to be without. To discover what these books
would be, imagine that you are going to a south sea island for
five years. What books would you take with you? I looked

over my list and put asterisks (*) next to those books I wanted to take with me. These special books are lifelong teachers and companions.

III. OTHER BOOKS. Below is a list of additional works that relate to the topics in this book. There are two criteria I used in selecting these books. The book and/or author (1) had given me something I valued, and (2) was an important stepping-stone for some friend or associate of mine.

EDUCATION, PHILOSOPHY & LIVING

Barnes, Hazel E. *Existentialist Ethics*. Knopf.
Cassirer, Ernest. *Essay on Man*. Bantam.
Dewey, John. *A Common Faith*. Yale.
      Art as Experience. Putnam.
Fadiman, James, ed. *The Proper Study of Man: Perspectives on the Social Sciences*. Macmillan.
Friedman, Maurice. *The Problematic Rebel*. University of Chicago.
Goodman, Paul. *Growing up Absurd*. Random House.
Hammarskjold, Dag. *Markings*. Knopf.
Kazantzakis, Nikos. *The Last Temptation of Christ*. Bantam.
      The Fratricides. Cassier.
Krutch, Joseph Wood. *Human Nature and the Human Condition*. Random House.
Leonard, George. *Education and Ecstasy*. Delacorte.
      The Transformation. Delacorte.
McGlashan, Alan. *The Savage and The Beautiful Country*. Houghton-Mifflin.
The Autobiography of Malcolm X. Grove.
Montessori, Maria. *The Discovery of the Child*. Ballantine.
Mumford, Louis. *Conduct of Life*. Harcourt, Brace & World.
Murphy, Michael. *Golf in the Kingdom*. Viking.
Neill, A. S. *Summerhill*. Hart.
Riesman, David. *The Lonely Crowd*. Yale.
Turnbull, Colin. *The Forest People*. Simon & Schuster.
Wilson, Colin. *Beyond the Outsider*. Houghton-Mifflin.

ORGANIC LIVING

Some of the most interesting stumbling around recently has been our attempt to regain the values of simpler life styles. These activities are the result of an awareness of two factors: (1) growth is a unified process; (2) through our cleverness we have manipulated, controlled, and preserved ourselves into a place where we are endangering our environment and our awareness of nature. I know of no book directly on this subject. However, many who are synthesizing the process of spiritual, personal, and physical growth rely upon the following volumes as guides for specific parts of their quests:

Davis, Adelle. *Let's Eat Right to Keep Fit*. New American Library.

Hunter, Beatrice Trum. *Consumer Beware!* Simon and Schuster.

Jefferson, Thomas. *Garden Book*. American Philosophical Society.

Langer, Richard W. *Grow It!* Avon.

Lappé, Frances Moore. *Diet For a Small Planet*. Ballantine.

Nearing, Helen and Scott. *Living the Good Life*. Schocken.

Rodale, J. I., ed. *The Encyclopedia of Organic Gardening*. Rodale Books.

PSYCHOLOGY & SCIENCE

Allport, Gordon. *Becoming: Basic Considerations for a Psychology of Personality*. Yale.

Ardrey, Robert. *The Territorial Imperative*. Atheneum.

Assagioli, Roberto. *Psychosynthesis*. Viking.

Bronowski, Jacob. *The Identity of Man*. Doubleday.

Erikson, Erik H. *Identity and the Life Cycle*. International University.

Faraday, Ann. *Dream Power*. Coward.

Frankl, Viktor. *Man's Search for Meaning*. Beacon.

Freud, Sigmund. *General Introduction to Psychoanalysis*. Pocket Books.

Fromm, Erich. *Escape from Freedom*. Avon.
    Man for Himself. Fawcett.
Horney, Karen. *New Ways in Psychoanalysis*. Norton.
Jourard, Sidney. *Transparent Self*. Van Nostrand.
Kubler-Ross, Elizabeth. *On Death and Dying*. Macmillan.
Laing, Ronald D. *The Divided Self*. Penguin.
    The Politics of Experience. Ballantine.
Lilly, John C. *The Center of the Cyclone*. Julian Press.
Lowen, Alexander. *Betrayal of the Body*. Macmillan.
Malinowski, Bronislaw. *Magic, Science & Religion*. Doubleday.
May, Rollo. *Love and Will*. Norton.
    Man's Search for Himself. New American Library.
Moustakas, Clark E. *Loneliness*. Prentice-Hall.
Naranjo, Claudio and Ornstein, Robert. *On the Psychology of Meditation*. Viking.
Oswald, Ian. *Sleep*. Penguin.
Pearson, Leonard, ed. *Death and Dying: Current Issues in the Treatment of the Dying Person*. Case Western University.
Peterson, Severin. *A Catalogue of the Ways People Grow*. Ballantine.
Progoff, Ira. *Depth Psychology and Modern Man*. Julian Press.
    Jung's Psychology and Its Social Meaning. Julian Press.
Schutz, William. *Joy: Expanding Human Awareness*. Grove.
Stevens, John O. *Awareness*. Real People.
Sullivan, Harry S. *Fusion of Psychiatry and Social Science*. Norton.
    Interpersonal Theory of Psychiatry. Norton.
Sutich, A. J. and Vich, M. A., eds. *Readings in Humanistic Psychology*. Free Press.
Szasz, Thomas. *Myth of Mental Illness*. Dell.
Tart, Charles, ed. *Altered States of Consciousness*. Wiley.

SPIRITUAL GROWTH

The Works of Aelred of Rievaulx. Cistercian Publications.
Argüelles, José and Miriam. *Mandala*. Shambala.
Aurelius, Marcus, *Meditations*. Gateway.
Bonhoeffer, Dietrich. *Letters and Papers from Prison*. Macmillan.

Buber, Martin. *Knowledge of Man*. Maurice Friedman, ed. Harper.
    I and Thou. Scribner.
Chadhuri, Haridas. *Integral Yoga*. George Allen & Unwin.
Feng, Gia-Fu and Kirk, Jerome. *Tai Chi—A Way of Centering and I Ching*. Collier.
Gibran, Kahil. *The Prophet*. Knopf.
    The Madman. Knopf.
Huxley, Aldous. *Doors of Perception*. Harper.
    Perennial Philosophy. Harper.
Huxley, Laura. *You Are Not the Target*. Wilshire Book.
James, William. *Principles of Psychology*. Dover.
    Varieties of Religious Experience. New American Library.
Keen, Sam. *To a Dancing God*. Harper.
Kennett, Jiyu. *Selling Water by the River*. Vintage.
Krishnamurti, J. *Think on These Things*. Harper.
Tillich, Paul. *The Courage to Be*. Yale.
Watts, Alan. *Way of Zen*. Random House.
    The Book. Collier.

AN AFTERWORD . . .

I appreciate the many individuals who have made this book possible.

My greatest and most joyful debt is to Sister Mary Martha whose commitment to the book has been equal to my own. She worked with me step by step and was often instrumental in my going on at difficult moments. Through her encouragement, prodding, and critical evaluation, this work has seen the light of day.

The book has greatly benefited from the editorial attention of my wife, Claire McCarroll, and my good friend Elizabeth Gardiner. They have patiently used their professional skills in tidying up my rough offspring.

These pages arose from my experiences in the unique environment of the Humanist Institute. It was here that I took major steps in my own growth. I feel especially appreciative to those with whom I have worked most closely; my fellow facilitators and the Residents at the Humanist Institute and all my other companions in The Community of The Simple Life.

I am indebted to the dozens of people with whom I have been privileged to share the intimate circle of a "Me Group." Thank you all for traveling in my inner world and giving me a passport to travel in yours.

TOLBERT MCCARROLL
April 1974
San Francisco